MAKE YOUR MONEY WORK

Rosemary Burr

Sponsored by Save & Prosper

Published by ROSTERS LTD.
60 Welbeck Street, London W1

© Rosemary Burr
ISBN 0 9480 3211 1

First Edition 1987

Designed and published by ROSTERS
Typeset by Gwynne Printers Ltd, Hurstpierpoint, Sussex
Printed and bound in Great Britain by Cox & Wyman Ltd, Reading

INTRODUCTION

Everyone wants to make the most they can from their hard earned cash, but how should they go about it? Nowadays it seems everywhere you go there are people eager to tell you what to do with **your** money. New products are launched almost daily and it is difficult to keep track of them, let alone formulate any overall plan.

This book starts by going back to basics. It looks at what **you** want to achieve and shows you how to arrange your affairs to maximise your chances of financial success. There are plenty of checklists and tables to help you tailor the general advice to your own circumstances and suggestions of when you will need to overhaul your financial arrangements.

Here at Save & Prosper we have been advising individuals how best to look after their savings and investments for over 50 years. More than 500,000 people trust us with their money. We offer a wide range of investments: high interest bank accounts, pension plans, unit trusts, personal equity plans and share dealing services through our stockbroking subsidiary. In order to gain maximum benefit from our range of products it is vital that people plan their investments. We hope this book will put them on the road to better financial planning.

Save & Prosper, September 1987.

Acknowledgements

A great number of people have helped me put together the information and statistics for this book. They have done so with patience and good humour. Save & Prosper, who sponsored the book, have been a marvellous source of data, advice and guidance, although I think they sometimes wondered when I would stop asking questions and finish writing.

Many other companies and organisations have also provided me with vital assistance. They include:

AA
Abbey National Building Society

Barclays Bank
Building Societies Association

Inland Revenue
ISIS

Legal and General Assurance

Midland Bank
Money Management

National Savings
Norwich Union

Prudential

Quilter Goodison

Unit Trust Association

My thanks to them all.

Contents

CHAPTER ONE:
WHY PLAN

If someone handed you a wadge of fifty pound notes and suggested you toss them out of the window, you would think that person was mad. However, every day people take decisions about what to do with their money which while not as blatantly daft as chucking it out the window are in fact equally stupid in terms of their own needs and circumstances.

Perhaps this sounds a little harsh. Well, consider the facts:

Fact One: Nearly half the families in this country have no life assurance

Fact Two: Roughly two thirds of our retired population rely on the state, family or friends for cash

Fact Three: About 30% of the nation's savings are tucked away in banks, building societies and National Savings where there is no opportunity for the money to grow.

In short, we work hard to earn our money and then all too often give little or no thought about what to do with the cash. Of course, there are many more interesting and enjoyable pursuits than trying to pick the right insurance policy or calculating the benefits from a pension plan, but it really does pay to spend a little time planning your financial affairs. Indeed, many people actually find once they start delving into the world of shares and investments that it is quite fascinating. Even if you do not fall into this category you will reap the benefits in terms of both more peace of mind and hopefully a more prosperous future.

11

Starting line

At this point you may be thinking, well that sounds fine in principle but how can I afford to save? You probably have the same sort of wallet as I have – the type with the invisible hole through which all the money that was meant to be there has somehow slipped away. If so, do not despair, this book is not about counting pennies, but working out how you can invest and save your money in order to enjoy more pounds in the future.

Earnings capacity

First of all let us consider the amount of cash that is likely to pass through your hands during a normal working life of forty-five years. Table One will give you a good idea of the staggering sums involved. Let us take as an example a thirty-five year old earning £15,000 a year. To date he or she will have earned £126,000 pounds and over the rest of his or her working life can expect to earn a further £997,000. Making a grand total take-home pay of over one million pounds – £1,123,000 to be exact.

The figures have been calculated on a fairly conservative basis, using as a starting point the current salary, i.e. in the above case £15,000. Certain assumptions had then to be made about the individual's past earnings history and future prospects. The figures for the past years have been based on recent wage experience. For those under thirty earnings to date assume that the individual received a pay rise of 5% each year to bring them up to their current take-home pay. For those over thirty, a wage rise of 10% has been used to mirror the higher wage hikes in the past thirty years when inflation was often running at double figures. The stream of future earnings has assumed pay rises of 5% each year, which is in line with current pay negotiations.

Here's a quick test you can try for yourself to see how you are faring in the money stakes. Take the figure which resembles most closely your total earnings to date and compare this with the balance in your bank or building society

Table One: Estimated Earnings During Working Life

Age	£10,000	£15,000	£20,000	£25,000	
		CURRENT SALARY			
25	£45,000	£68,000	£91,000	£114,000	To date
	£1,208,000	£1,812,000	£2,416,000	£3,020,000	In future
35	£84,000	£126,000	£167,000	£209,000	To date
	£664,000	£997,000	£1,329,000	£1,661,000	In future
45	£100,000	£150,000	£200,000	£250,000	To date
	£331,000	£496,000	£661,000	£827,000	In future
55	£106,000	£159,000	£212,000	£265,000	To date
	£126,000	£189,000	£252,000	£314,000	In future

Source: Save & Prosper. July 1987

account plus any other investments. How do they compare? If your investments and savings are less than 10% you need to do better in future. This will give you a rough and ready idea of whether or not your earnings have been put to good use or swallowed up to finance daily living.

Money multiplier

You do not need to save a large proportion of your money in order to build up a cash sum. Let us take as an example a fifty-five year old man now earning £15,000 a year. If that person manages to save just 5% of his current pay each year, i.e. £750, and invests in a product which produces growth of 10% net per year he will build up a nest egg of £13,148 by the time he reaches retirement age.

If the same person had managed to squirrel away £2,000 and obtained 10% net per annum then the lump sum would have been boosted to £35,062. The key point to remember is that 'money makes money'.

Financial planning is a matter of sorting out your priorities and deciding how best to use your cash. You may prefer to spend all your money today and give no thought to next year's holiday or how much income you will have on

13

retirement. However, when you see how relatively small sums invested today can grow in the future you may decide after all that you can afford to invest a small percentage of your current earnings.

Table Two: How the Money Grows

Sum per month	5 years	After 10 years	15 years	20 years	25 years
£20	1,543.43	4,029.43	8,032.39	14,479.64	24,862.99
£50	3,858.57	10,073.57	20,080.97	36,199.1	62,157.47
£100	7,717.15	20,147.14	40,161.94	72,398.20	124,315.94
£200	15,434.30	40,294.30	80,323.90	144,796.40	248,629.90
£500	38,585.70	100,735.70	200,809.70	361,991.00	621,574.70

Note: The calculations assume a net return after basic rate tax of 10% per annum.

Source: Save & Prosper.

Table Two shows how quickly relatively small sums invested each month can grow. It assumes that your money grows at the rate of 10% net.

Personal checklist

Planning your financial affairs need not be painful. In fact, the whole process is designed to make sure you get full value for your money. It is a very personal exercise and must depend not only on your own needs and wishes but also any family obligations. You may wish to retire early, to finance a holiday home abroad or build up a cash sum to start your own business.

Sometimes in the past investment companies and their sales force have been concerned with selling specific products rather than giving overall planning guidance. However, under the new rules introduced by the Financial Services Act (1986) which are expected to come into force in January 1988, companies, their representatives and independent investment advisers will be required to show that they have tailored their advice to suit the customer's overall requirements and keep a record of why specific products were recommended.

That said, you will greatly increase your chance of obtaining the best advice on specific products if you work out in advance three things:

- your current financial profile
- your short term needs
- your long term requirements

First, you will need to build up a picture of your present financial position. It is probably best to set aside an afternoon to do this. Table Three is designed to help you work out your family's cash flow after the taxman has taken his bite and Table Four to show you how much you have accumulated to date.

The crucial figure here is after-tax spending power. This exercise is doubly useful as not only will it establish your family's cash flow position but it will also highlight your tax payments. An important part of financial planning is minimising your tax liability by making sure you are investing in the best type of products to suit your tax bracket.

Do not worry if you cannot obtain the exact figures at this stage. By simply filling in this table you will get a snap shot picture of your family's current financial health. Then deduct your outgoings from your income after tax and the result will be the sum of money you have left to spend on extras or invest.

Table Three: Family Cash Flow for Past Tax Year*

	Gross	After Tax
a) Incoming		
Income		
Salary		
Yours		
Wife/Husband		
Children		
Commission/Bonuses		
Pension		
Investment income		
Interest		
Dividends from shares		
Distributions from unit trusts		
Income from insurance policies		
Rental income		
Capital gains		
From sales of investments		
Sale of other goods		
Lump sums		
Gifts		
Inheritance		
Redundancy		
Total income		

Table Three: Family Cash Flow for Past Tax Year* – Continued

	Gross	After Tax
b) Outgoings *General household expenses*		
Interest payments		
Bank loans		
Credit cards		
Hire purchase		
Mortgage		
Other		
Total		
Insurance		
Home and contents		
Motor		
Life		
Health		
Other		
Total		
Regular savings or investment		
Tax		
Income tax		
Capital gains tax		
Inheritance tax		
Other		
Grand Total		

*The tax year starts on April 6.

Table Four: What is Your Family Worth?*

	£
a) What you own	
Ready money	
Cash in bank	
Cash in building societies	
Other cash deposits	
Investments which could be sold immediately	
Shares	
Unit trusts	
Share options	
Government securities	
Personal Equity Plans	
Long term investments	
Insurance policies	
Pension entitlements	
Friendly society plans	
Shares in unquoted companies	
Holdings in Business Expansion Schemes	
Property	
Your main residence	
Other homes	
Personal goods	
Car	
Contents of your home	
Jewellery	
Other	
Total	

Notes: the ready money section covers your savings, i.e. cash on which you earn interest but where you can withdraw the full sum whenever you wish, subject to any requirement to give a period of notice. Investments which could be sold immediately cover those products which are easy to buy or sell without involving you in major financial penalties or extra tax bills. Long term investments are those which would either be difficult to sell straight away, perhaps because there is no market in the shares, i.e. in the case of unquoted companies, or because you would suffer a tax penalty, i.e. on some insurance and friendly society plans.

Table Four: What is Your Family Worth?* – Continued

	£
b) What you owe	
Unpaid bills	
Short term borrowings	
Bank loans	
Hire purchase	
Store credit	
Credit card debt	
Long term borrowings	
Home loan	
Business loans	
Others	
Total	

The difference between what you own and what you owe represents your family fortune.

Together the infomation on these two tables will help you determine:

- how much spare cash you have to invest
- whether you are paying too much tax
- whether you are borrowing in the most efficient way
- whether you are taking full advantage of the tax incentives involved in long term investments
- how vulnerable you are to any abrupt changes in income
- whether your investments are reasonably distributed to meet your current needs
- whether you are investing for the right balance between income and capital
- how your outgoings would respond to any changes in interest rates
- whether you have sufficient insurance to match the value of your assets
- how successful you have been in recent years in building up your family's wealth

So much for the past, now we turn to the future. Table

Table Five: Current Priorities

	£
Home	
Move to larger property	
Improve current property	
Buy second home	
Recreational	
Buy boat	
Go on holiday	
Buy sporting equipment	
Educational	
School fees	
University fees	
Part time education	
Family	
Increase size of family	
Switch to part time work	
Become self employed	
Change lifestyle	
Total	

Five gives a sample checklist of your medium term priorities.
You will probably wish to devise your own list but this will
give you some idea of how it is done.

For the moment do not worry too much about the exact
costs involved. Just try and work out what you would like to
achieve or do in the coming years. Some options will require
a cash sum, such as home improvements or a second home,
while others will be a matter of trying to build up a stream

of income over future years, i.e. to fund school fees or pay for a growing family.

Once you have worked out your medium term aims turn your attention to the future., Your checklist may contain some of the items we have listed in Table Five plus additions covering retirement, supporting elderly parents or grown up children and ensuring your assets are passed onto other members of your family in the most tax efficient way.

You should now have a good picture of your finances annd equally important what it is you wish to achieve. The following chapters will show you the various ways you can build up a cash sum, provide an income and arrange your affairs to minimise your tax bill.

CHAPTER TWO:
BUYING A LITTLE PROTECTION

Financial planning is concerned with reducing your money worries in the future and giving you the cash resources to enjoy the lifestyle you have chosen. Before we look at how to accumulate more money it is vitally important to remember that the first step in planning your affairs should be to protect what you have already achieved. Just as a castle built on unsecure foundations will topple down, so the whole process of planning can come to a sticky end if we do not first make certain that we have adequately insured our existing income and assets.

Income standby

Most of us rely on our current earnings to pay for our food, clothing and shelter. If our income from this source suddenly dried up tomorrow we would find it virtually impossible to maintain our present standard of living for more than a few months at best. We may be able to live off our savings supplemented by a small amount of investment income but probably not for long.

So what can we do to protect ourselves from this devastating loss of income? The answer is quite a lot, depending on why the income tap has been cut off.

● Ill health

You can protect up to 75% of your current income between the time you fall ill until you would have retired by buying what is called rather strangely Permanent Health Insurance.

It is permanent in the sense that once the insurance company has agreed to provide you with the cover it cannot reverse that decision regardless of what subsequently happens to your state of health.

The cost of these policies varies tremendously, depending on the level of benefits, your job and your sex. As a rough rule of thumb the younger you are, the safer your job, then the cheaper the policy. Also, the majority of companies charge women up to 50% more than their male counterparts for this type of plan. This the insurance companies say is based on past claims experience. A fact hotly contested by a number of newer companies and some friendly societies.

Apart from the size of the eventual payments, three other factors which come into play on the benefit side are whether you are prepared to defer drawing money under a policy for the first weeks of illness, whether you are looking for increased benefits over the years to protect yourself against any rises in inflation and whether you wish to insure against being unable to perform a specific job, e.g. a football player will need very specific cover, since if he cannot play football, he may not be able to earn a similar sum elsewhere. He might not however be permanently disabled in the terms of a Permanent Health Insurance contract. Obviously if you agree to delay any claims for a certain period of time and are willing to receive a fixed sum over the rest of your normal working life the policy is cheaper than if you request a growing income and immediate payment.

Table One shows you some examples of the costs per month based on a benefit £7,000 per annum and indicates how these can alter quite dramatically depending on your circumstances. You should pay particular attention to the deferment period as under your terms of employment you should be covered for short bouts of ill health. If you are self-employed you will probably be wise to pay rather more for the security of knowing you can start receiving an income within say eight weeeks rather tha opt for the cheaper version which will leave a six month gap. The proceeds of your policy will normally be taxed as income in your hands. However, as a special concession the payment is not taxed unless and until you have received payments for a full tax year, which starts on April 5.

If you think the premiums on a Permanent Health Insurance policy are too steep for you at present but would still like to buy some cover in the case of short term illness, there are a number of alternatives. Table Two shows you the costs of purchasing what is called personal accident and sickness cover, which will give you an income or cash sum in certain defined circumstances. You buy these policies on an annual basis which means the insurance company will set the rate you have to pay each year depending on your circumstances at the time.

The cost and specific conditions of each company's personal accident policy differ. They cover you against a range of pre-defined accidents, mostly the sort that happen at work, at home or on the road plus they provide you with an element of life cover. The cost is based solely on your occupation and the level of benefits taken. It is possible to buy accident cover for housewives and children as well as those in employment.

To give you an example of the costs and benefits we have examined the policy available from the Prudential. They divide the working population into six categories of varying degrees of risk, starting at 'one' for the secretaries, teachers and accountants rising to 'six' for dockers, tower crane drivers and railway track maintenance staff. They also quote for the rest of the family. Table Two shows how the costs vary for a standard package which would pay:

- £20,000 on death
- £20,000 for the loss of a limb or eye
- £20,000 for total disability
- £40 per week for temporary total disability
- £20 per week for temporary partial disability
- £5 per day hospitalisation benefit

The temporary total disability payment is not available to anyone not in paid employment, i.e. it is excluded from housewives' and chldrens' policies. Children are not covered

Table One: The Costs of Permanent Health Insurance

(a) Men in low risk jobs		
Age	Deferred period in weeks	Monthly premium (£)
35	13	12.15
45	13	17.96
35	26	9.56
45	26	14.04
35	52	8.02
45	52	11.66

(b) Men in higher risk jobs		
Age	Deferred period in weeks	Monthly premium (£)
35	13	18.03
45	13	23.91
35	26	13.69
45	26	18.17
35	52	12.15
45	52	15.79

(c) Women in low risk jobs		
Age	Deferred period in weeks	Monthly premium (£)
35	13	18.51
45	13	23.28
35	26	12.08
45	26	18.03
35	52	10.05
45	52	14.88

(d) Women in low risk jobs		
Age	Deferred period in weeks	Monthly premium (£)
35	13	21.39
45	13	29.23
35	26	16.21
45	26	22.16
35	52	14.18
45	52	19.01

Source: Prudential Corporation, June, 1987.

Notes:
1. Low risk jobs are professions such as solicitors plus bank managers and clerical staff. higher risk jobs include heavy manual workers, engineers, etc.
2. Quotes are based on a benefit of £7,000 per annum payable every four weeks in arrears.
3. Premiums are bsed on deferred period selected, i.e. waiting thirteen, twenty-six or fifty-two weeks before receiving payment.
4. Benefit payable up to retirement at sixty-five.

for temporary partial disability and the hospital benefit is reduced to £2.50 per week.

Table Two: Comparative Cost of Standard Accident Assurance Package

Category	Cost Per Annum (£)
1	30
2	40
3	60
4	80
5	110
6	150
Spouse	60
Children	20

Source: Prudential June, 1987

- **Class 1**
  Accountant
  Bank staff
  Clerk (office or shop)
  Draughtsman
  Secretary
  Teacher

- **Class 2**
  Bus inspector
  Cafe proprietor
  Hospital nurse
  Painter and Decorator (interior)
  Shopkeeper/assistant
  Traffic Warden
  Photographer (no premises)

- **Class 3**
  Ambulance driver/attendant
  Bus driver/conductor
  Caretaker
  Electrician (domestic/office)
  Garage Mechanic
  Roundsman (bread, laundry, milk)

- **Class 4**
  Boatbuilder
  Bricklayer
  Carpenter/Joiner
  Fireman
  Plumber

- **Class 5**
  Boilerman
  Bricklayer's Mate
  Carpenter's Mate
  Farm Worker
  Quarry Worker

- **Class 6**
  Docker
  Railway track maintenance staff
  Tower Crane Driver (Construction Industry)

A good financial adviser will be able to help you choose the best type of product and in turn the best value for money policy to suit your needs. Always ask for several competing quotes with a clear indication not just of the benefits but any exclusion clauses. Only then can you weigh up the relative costs in terms of the amount of cover you will be getting. Often what looks at first glance to be the cheapest policy, turns out on closer inspection to give fairly poor value per pound of premium.

28

• Redundancy cover

Unfortunately you cannot buy an insurance policy which will replace your income if you are made redundant. If you think you fall into the high risk category there are a few steps you can take to reduce the level of income you will need to continue to support your current lifestyle. You can buy what is called redundancy cover on your mortgage and most bank loans. If you are subsequently made redundant then the interest payments on these debts will be paid for a specified period, normally up to two years. This at least gives you a breathing space and may reduce your outgoings by up to 60% depending on your circumstances.

These policies are quite expensive, for example, in June 1987 if you took out a one year £1,000 personal loan from the Midland Bank the cost of protecting yourself against unemployment, sickness and death would be £57, and this sum would have been automatically included in your repayments unless you specifically requested the cover to be excluded. Many finance companies now include this type of cover as a matter of course and leave the onus on you, the borrower, to opt out. As with all types of legal agreements it pays to read the small print.

Income replacement

Most of us would agree with Woody Allen when he said, "I don't mind dying - as long as I'm not there at the time". The problem arises when this mental block results in our families and relatives being left unprotected. It is a sad but true fact that as a nation the British are woefully underinsured. While the Americans, for example, will boast about the amount of life cover they have we English prefer to sweep the whole issue under the carpet.

The first step is to work out how much life cover you need and then to look at the various ways your requirements can be met. Finally, you want to buy the right product to suit your age, income and family circumstances. Tables Three and Four will help you do this. Table Three itemises the sums

Table Three: Income Replacement Planner

To use this table add your capital requirements to the lump sum you need to provide your monthly income and deduct any payments received.

a) Capital requirements

Item	£
Outstanding mortgage	_____
Hire purchase	_____
Credit cards	_____
Other debts	_____
Funeral expenses	_____
Solicitors	_____
Total a)	_____

b) Monthly income requirements

Item	£
Household expenditure	_____
Clothing	_____
Car	_____
Holidays	_____
Education	_____
Life Assurance	_____
Total b)	_____
Minus any monthly income (state benefits, investment income etc.)	_____
Total monthly income	_____
Lump sum required to provide monthly income*	_____

c) Payments received

Item	£
Pension lump sum	_____
Life assurance	_____
Mortgage protection	_____
Other	_____
Total c)	_____

*Use Table Four to select the appropriate lump sum.

you will need to pay off any outstanding debts plus funeral costs as well as looking at the amount of monthly income you require. If you have filled in the tables on your family income and what your family is worth in chapter one then you should find this table easy to complete. The one item you will not be able to write in straight away is the one asterisked, i.e. lump sum required to provide monthly income. To work out that figure you will need to use Table Four: The Sum Assured Selector. This will help you convert your income needs into an appropriate lump sum requirement. It is based on the assumption that a given lump of capital will produce an annual income each year of 8% net of tax. The annual income has been divided into twelve monthly payments to help you fill in Table Three.

Table Four: Sum Assured Selector

Monthly income required	Sum assured to maintain indicated monthly income assuming a net investment return of 8%
£ 200	£ 30,696
£ 300	£ 46,044
£ 400	£ 61,044
£ 500	£ 76,740
£ 600	£ 92,089
£ 700	£107,437
£ 800	£122,785
£ 900	£138,133
£1,000	£153,481

Notes:
The figures shown above assume a net investment return.
Monthly income is assumed to be payable monthly in advance.

Source: Save & Prosper, July 1987.

Once you have filled out Table Three you can work out how much life assurance you require. You need to add your capital requirements (column (a)) to the lump sum required to provide your monthly income and finally deduct any payments you would receive (column (c)). The figure you reach indicates the amount of life assurance you need to purchase to support your family's existing lifestyle.

Table Five: Life Assurance Needs

	£
Capital requirements	_____
Lump sum to replace income	_____
Total	_____
Minus cash received	_____
Life assurance need	_____

Now that you have worked out how much cover you require, the time has come to look at the type of products on the market which can satisfy your need. There are basically three ways you can buy life assurance. The first and cheapest is called term. You buy a certain sum of cover for a fixed term. Second, and slightly more expensive is something called whole life. Here you buy a certain level of cover but provided you continue to pay the premiums it will pay out whenever you die. Third, and most expensive is a hybrid policy called endowment. This is effectively a combination of life assurance and investment. It provides you with a given amount of life assurance cover for a fixed period and a lump sum at the end of the period if you survive which is related to the investment return on your premiums.

So which is the right policy for you? If your resources are limited, perhaps because you are just starting a family and have taken on a hefty mortgage and you are still relatively young then term assurance is usually the best bet. If you can afford the higher cost of whole life assurance then by starting such a policy relatively young you may be able to reduce the level of premiums you have to pay during the latter part of your life. That is because the cost is calculated on the basis

32

Table Six: Comparative Monthly Costs of Life Assurance

Type of insurance	Age 29 Male £	Female £	Age 39 Male £	Female £	Age 49 Male £	Female £
20 year term policy	3.70	3.20	8.45	6.45	22.95	16.95
whole life policy*	42.20	38.95	64.95	59.45	126.45	115.70
20 year endowment policy**	108.95	108.70	112.70	111.20	124.20	119.45

Notes:
1. The table is based on figures supplied by the Norwich Union in January 1987.
2. In each case the sum insured is £25,000 and the buyer is a healthy, non-smoker.
3. Customers who choose either whole life policies or endowments will receive a lump sum when the policy pays out. The exact size of this lump sum will be determined by the insurance company's investment performance. As a guide we list below the sums you would receive if the insurance company produced a return of 10.75% per annum on your money. This estimate has been calculated according to industry guidelines introduced in the autumn of 1986.

  *£204,958 for a twenty-nine year old, assuming death thirty-five years later.
  £79,460 for a thirty-nine year old, assuming death twenty years later.
  £79,460 for a forty-nine year old, assuming death twenty years later.
  **£79,460 for a with-profits policy.

of your age when you first take out the whole life policy. Another advantage of whole life policies is that most can be adjusted to pay out rising benefits over the years. The plans are sometimes costed so that if you are lucky enough to live beyond seventy-five years old you do not have to pay any more premiums after that date.

Endowment policies are suitable for older people who wish to achieve two aims: to build up a lump sum if they survive and to provide a minimum level of support for their family if they die. They can also be useful as a way of paying off certain large debts such as a mortgage. However, people who purchase endowment policies to pay off their mortgage usually link the size of the policy quite naturally to the amount of the mortgage, rather than working out their genuine insurance needs. This means they will not have the correct amount of life assurance and may end up buying additional cover when they are older at a higher price.

Life assurance policies can be useful in general tax planning as we shall see in more detail later. That is because the lump sum you receive is free of tax in your hands. However, if you opt for an endowment policy remember that your investment has already been taxed by the government. Insurance companies pay corporation tax, currently 35%, on any capital gains they make by investing your money and that will be reflected in your ultimate pay-out. Also, when choosing an endowment plan remember that the value of the lump sum if you survive will depend on the investment skill of the insurance company you choose as well as the general state of stock markets during the period they have invested your premiums, if it is what is called a with-profits plan, or the actual level of the stock market when you cash in your policy if it is unit-linked.

Table Seven shows just how much this variation in share prices can affect your payment when the endowment plan matures. We have looked at the top five performing ten year with-profit plans maturing at various times over the past decade. The table shows both the actual lump sum pay-out you would have received and then what percentage of this amount was given as a special final bonus to reflect the state of share prices at that time. More recently this emphasis on final bonuses has been taken to an even greater extreme. Some plans maturing in the Spring of this year have been boosted by bonuses larger than the amount built up over the whole ten year period.

Table Seven: Comparative Performance of Ten Year With-Profits Policies

Maturity	1978			1981		
	£	%		£	%	
Equitable	1,194	9.1	Equitable	1,996	13.0	
London Life	1,834	10.3	London Life	1,970	13.6	
RNPFN	1,812	3.8	RNPFN	1,947	4.1	
Post Office	1,810	—	Post Office	1,917	—	
NALGO	1,797	7.5	Friends Provident	1,877	12.0	
1983			**1984**			
	£	%		£	%	
Equitable	2,078	14.9	Ecclesiastical	2,263	23.1	
Ecclesiastical	2,072	17.4	Equitable	2,258	21.6	
Scottish Widows	2,060	18.0	Standard Life	2,255	27.3	
London Life	2,053	15.4	Norwich Union	2,249	24.1	
UK Provident	2,053	15.5	Scottish Widows	2,235	23.7	

Notes: Based on true gross premium of £10 per month. Policy purchased by a man aged thirty at next birthday.

Source: Money Management, May 1987.

So while endowment plans may have a role in your financial strategy, picking the right one is bound to be difficult. You should look for a consistently strong investment performance not one which has been boosted by large one-off bonuses.

CHAPTER THREE:
COVERING YOUR ASSETS

Most people's biggest asset, aside from their earning power, is their home. If you have a mortgage then the lender normally insists you buy insurance to cover the property and will usually present you with a short list of insurance companies from which to choose. If you opt for a different insurance company from those on the list you will usually be charged an extra so-called administrative fee of up to £25. The lender reserves the right to turn down your choice of company if they are not satisfied with the level of cover provided, but this is quite a rare occurrence.

As with all general insurance, i.e. that covering things, rather than people, you should aim to pick not the cheapest policy but the one which gives you best value for money. This is difficult to measure but you should look at the extent of cover you are being offered, often only gauged by reading the small print listing the exclusions, as well as the company's record for settling claims swiftly and fairly. One advantage of opting for a company on the lender's short list is that if you need to claim you can usually rely on the lender's muscle with the insurer to help speed your claim through the system.

Contrary to what many people believe you do not insure a building for its current worth or even its future value, but rather for the cost of rebuilding it. Most policies will pay the full cost of any necessary repairs or rebuilding provided you have insured the property for the correct sum and not let its condition deteriorate. However some policies, which may appear cheaper on the surface, will make deductions for wear and tear. That means if the rebuilt home is in better condition

Table One: Rebuilding Costs

How much would it cost to re-build your home? September 1986 costings – £ per square foot (external)

		PRE 1920			1920 – 1945			1946 – DATE		
		LARGE	MEDIUM	SMALL	LARGE	MEDIUM	SMALL	LARGE	MEDIUM	SMALL
DETACHED HOUSE	Region 1	53.00	57.00	56.00	50.50	52.50	53.00	43.00	45.50	46.00
	2	46.50	50.00	49.00	44.50	46.00	46.50	37.50	40.00	40.00
	3	44.00	47.50	46.50	42.00	44.00	44.00	36.00	38.00	38.00
	4	41.50	45.00	44.00	40.00	41.50	41.50	34.00	36.00	36.00
	Typical Area ft²	3450	1700	1300	2550	1350	1050	2550	1350	1050
SEMI-DETACHED HOUSE	Region 1	51.50	52.50	52.50	54.50	52.50	52.50	39.00	41.50	44.50
	2	45.50	46.00	46.00	48.00	46.00	46.00	34.50	36.50	39.00
	3	43.00	44.00	43.50	45.50	44.00	44.00	32.50	34.50	37.00
	4	41.00	41.50	41.50	43.00	41.50	41.50	31.00	33.00	35.00
	Typical Area ft²	2300	1650	1200	1350	1150	900	1650	1350	1050
DETACHED BUNGALOW	Region 1	The chart does not cover pre-1920 bungalows, as few such properties were built.			54.50	50.50	52.00	47.00	47.00	49.00
	2				48.00	44.50	45.50	41.00	41.50	43.00
	3				45.50	42.00	43.00	39.00	39.50	41.00
	4				43.00	40.00	41.00	37.00	37.00	38.50
	Typical Area ft²				1650	1400	1000	2500	1350	1000
SEMI-DETACHED BUNGALOW	Region 1				56.50	57.00	50.50	45.50	46.00	47.50
	2				49.50	50.00	44.50	40.00	40.00	42.00
	3				47.00	47.50	42.00	38.00	38.00	39.50
	4				44.50	45.00	40.00	36.00	36.00	37.50
	Typical Area ft²				1350	1200	800	1350	1200	800
TERRACED HOUSE	Region 1	56.00	55.00	54.50	54.50	54.50	54.00	39.50	42.50	47.00
	2	49.00	48.00	48.00	48.00	47.50	47.00	34.50	37.50	41.50
	3	46.50	45.50	45.50	45.50	45.00	45.00	33.00	35.50	39.50
	4	44.00	43.50	43.00	43.00	43.00	42.50	31.00	33.50	37.00
	Typical Area ft²	1650	1350	1050	1350	1050	850	1650	1300	900

TABLE 1
REGIONS

1. London Boroughs
2. South East and North West England
   (Bedfordshire, Berkshire, Buckinghamshire, Essex, Hampshire, Hertfordshire, Kent, Oxfordshire, Surrey, East Sussex, West Sussex, Cheshire, Greater Manchester, Lancashire and Merseyside)
3. Scotland, Wales and Northern England
   (The whole of Scotland and Wales and Cleveland, Cumbria, Durham, Northumberland, Tyne & Wear)
4. East Anglia, East Midlands, West Midlands, South West, Yorkshire & Humberside and Northern Ireland
   (All other counties)

NOTES TO TABLE ONE

1. This chart has been prepared by the Building Cost Information Service of the Royal Institution of Chartered Surveyors and the majority of householders have been catered for by providing rebuilding cost information on five different house types, with average quality finish, depending on their age, size and location. Of course, it is impossible to cover all circumstances and, for instance, the chart is unsuitable for certain types of property including the following:
   (a) Properties which are not built mainly of brick.
   (b) Properties with more than two storeys (for three-storey houses, see 'Making your own estimate') or with basements and cellars.
   (c) Flats, because there are wide differences in construction and responsibilities for shared parts.
   (d) Houses with special design features or of greater sizes than those described in the chart.
2. **All the figures in the chart are based on houses of average quality finish and might need adjusting.** For example, if your house is of higher quality, with luxury kitchen and sanitary fittings, floor and wall finishes and double glazing, your final figure would need to be increased by up to 25%.
3. The figures in the chart are based on rebuilding your home to its existing standard using current materials and techniques available. If older houses are required to be reinstated in exactly their original style, a professional valuation is essential.
4. All the figures in the chart include allowances for full central heating (at an approximate cost of £2,200) and demolition costs and professional fees.

39

than your old one you will have to foot the bill for this improvement. These policies are rare now, but do watch out for them.

If you live in a leasehold flat then you should check the terms of your lease. In most cases the landlord is responsible for buying insurance cover for the whole block of flats and you will pay your portion through your maintenance charge. However, if you buy a converted flat from a builder or live in a maisonette you should ask the solicitor who is handling the conveyancing to check what insurance arrangements have been made and whose responsibility it is to maintain adequate cover. Those of you who have bought houses, whether freehold or leasehold, will be responsible for buying their own buildings cover.

Measuring up

The first step is to calculate how much buildings cover you need. This will depend not just on the size and type of property but also the estimated price of labour and materials in your area of the country. Tables One and Two will help you work out the figures for yourself, provided your house is of standard construction. This means it is built mainly of brick and consists of up to three storeys above ground. If you have installed double glazing, a luxury kitchen and de luxe bathroom then you should boost these average figures by up to 25%. Do not forget to add the cost of the garage, if necessary.

Table One gives a guide to the costs of rebuilding a range of properties in different parts of the country based on costings in September 1986. It has been prepared by the Building Cost Information Service of the Royal Institution of Chartered Surveyors. The table cannot be used for houses of more than four storeys, buildings with basements or cellars, buildings over one hundred and fifty years old or those of unusual construction, such as thatched roof cottages.

Table Two will help you work out the total cost. Depending on your dexterity with a tape measure, you may need help in measuring the dimensions of your home. If it is a new property then you should be able to work from the figures supplied by the builders and if you have purchased the house via an estate agent then they should be able to provide you with accurate figures. Failing that a reputable surveyor will be able to do the calculations for you.

First, start with the house itself. You need to work out the total floor area – upstairs and downstairs. Do not forget to take account to the space taken up by inside walls. If you have a three-storey house then you need only count 75% of the floor area of the top floor. This figure should be written in line A. You will fill in line B from the information supplied in Table One, depending on the type of property, its age and location. Line C shows the rebuilding cost of your house and is calculated by multiplying figure A by figure B. You then need to add in figures to take account of your garage and any other structures, such as fences. Put in your own estimates for these in line D and line E. This will give you a grand total for the approximate amount you should insure your property. Some policies will have a built-in escalation clause so your cover is automatically increased each year to take account of inflation, if not you will have to remember to do this yourself each year when you renew the policy.

Table Two: Estimated Buildings Cover Required

Line A	Total floor space (square feet)	
Line B	Rebuilding cost per square foot (see figures in Table One)	£
Line C	Estimated rebuilding cost of house (Multiply A×B)	£
Line D	Estimated cost of rebuilding garage	£
Line E	Estimated cost of other rebuilding	£
Total	C+D+E	£

Let us look at two examples, a terraced house in London

and a terraced house in Manchester of the same dimensions, 1,400 square feet.

Table Three: Estimated Buildings Cover of London Terraced House

Line A	Total floor space (square feet)	1400
Line B	Rebuilding costs per square foot	£56.00
Line C	Estimated rebuilding cost	£78,400
Line D	Estimated cost of rebuilding garage	Nil
Line E	Estimated cost of other rebuilding	Nil
Total		£78,400

Table Four: Estimated Buildings Cover of Machester Terraced House

Line A	Total floor space (square feet)	1400
Line B	Rebuilding costs per square foot	£49.00
Line C	Estimated rebuilding cost	£68,600
Line D	Estimated cost of rebuilding garage	Nil
Line E	Estimated cost of other rebuilding	Nil
Total		£68,600

The rebuilding costs were drawn from Table One, based on the region and size of the property. To be on the safe side, we took the figures for a large terraced house. London falls into region one, the most expensive in the country, while Manchester is included in region two. If we had moved our terrace house to the cheapest region in the country in terms of rebuilding costs, say Humberside, the estimated buildings cover required would have dropped dramatically to £61,600, i.e. 22% less than for the same property in London.

Do not forget to readjust the figures at a later date to take account of any home improvements, such as central heating,

42

new windows, upgrading your kitchen or bathroom, or building an extension.

Making your choice

If you live in a flat, your solicitor will be able to find out how much cover the landlord has purchased. By law the landlord has only to provide minimal cover and you should find out whether the policy covers problems with subsidence and water drainage. If you are not happy with the level of cover, you should try to get together with the other tenants and ask the landlord to extend it. After all, you will end up paying the bill through your maintenance charges.

Flat owners who wish to do their own thing and supplement the landlord's cover can choose two plans, the Knight Ellis and Co Flat Protection Plan and the Barnet Gold Leasehold Flat Indemnity Scheme. This top-up insurance will pay you the flat's market value if it is damaged by subsidence or water. If you cannot live in it temporarily it will pay towards the costs of alternative accommodation.

If you live in a house you can choose between:

- Basic buildings insurance cover

This will cover the structure of your home, e.g. foundations, walls, floors, doors, windows, roof, plumbing, decorations and insulation. Plus garages, sheds, patios, faces etc. It should also include permanent items which you could not take with you when you moved, except carpets which are regarded as part of your home's contents. The policy will pay the costs of repair on rebuilding if your home is damaged as a result of a specified list of causes, which will be stated in the policy. These normally include fire, storm, flood, subsidence, riot and water escaping from the plumbing or washing machine. However, in certain areas where subsidence or flooding is common these causes may be excluded and for certain types of property, i.e. thatched roof cottages, fire cover may be prohibitively expensive. If you accidentally damage the plumbing or sewage this should also be covered, but check.

Also included in this basic package should be payments towards temporary accommodation, usually up to 10% of the policy's value, towards professional fees involved in rebuilding and your public liability to other people, i.e. if a passer-by was hit by a slate falling off your roof during a storm.

● Extra accidental damage

For a higher fee you can buy a policy which will give you accidental damage cover against a much wider range of events. Again it is a matter of checking the fine print of each policy and weighing up the cost in relation to the amount of cover being given.

● Combined contents and insurance policy

As the name suggests, this is two types of cover in one. You work out the appropriate level of buildings cover in the usual way and then your contents are automatically insured for up to 50% of this sum.

Obviously if your contents are not worth nearly as much as 50% of your rebuilding costs you will be effectively paying

Table Five: Comparative Costs of Various Types of Home Insurance in Inner City Areas

Cover		Cost Per Annum			
Rebuilding cost	Contents value	Basic buildings cover	Extended* buildings cover	Contents cover	Combined buildings and contents
£ 40,000	£17,000	£72	£84	£204	£212
£ 50,000	£20,000	£90	£105	£240	£265
£ 60,000	£25,000	£108	£126	£300	£318
£100,000	£30,000	£180	£210	£360	£530

*includes additional accidental damage cover.

Notes: based on estimated insurance costs for illustative purposes of £1.80 per £1,000 basic buildings cover, £2.10 per £1,000 for extended buildings cover including accidental damage, £5.30 per £1,000 for the combined buildings and contents cover and £12.00 per £1,000 for contents cover alone.

for insurance you do not need. Table Five gives you a guide to comparative costs of different types of cover. The cost of the combined policy will vary according to region with higher risk areas such as inner cities being the most expensive.

You can work out the best value policy for your own circumstances by using Table Six.

Table Six: Home Insurance Planner

Line A	Buildings cover required	£ _____
Line B	Contents cover required	£ _____
Line C	Cost of basic building cover (Line A multiplied by £1.80)	£ _____
Line D	Cost of contents cover alone (Line C mutiplied by cost per thousand in your region)	£ _____
Line E	Combined cost of buying buildings and contents cover separately (Line C plus Line D)	£ _____
Line F	Costs of combined contents and buildings cover (Line A multiplied by £5.30)	£ _____

By comparing the sums in line E and line F you will be able to choose the best value for money. In order to complete this table you will need to know the value of your contents. Nearly everyone tends to underestimate this figure, especially as you should be insured for the full cost of replacing everything in your home. The best way to do this is to make a detailed list of the contents of each room in the house and get valuable items professionally valued. Table Seven will help you do this.

A word about contents policies, these come in a number of guises, and as with all insurance the greater the level of cover the higher the cost. In Table Five for comparative purposes we took the cost of insuring your contents based on the more expensive new for old rather than the old

Table Seven: Insuring your Contents – A Room by Room Guide

To find the value of your home contents enter your own estimated replacement values in the space provided.

SITTING ROOM	EXAMPLE NEW PRICE	YOUR ESTIMATE
Three piece suite, chairs	£800	£
TV and Video equipment	£750	£
Hi-Fi/personal computer	£450	£
Book case (including books), tables	£300	£
Cassettes, tapes and records	£250	£
Pictures, clocks, ornaments, lamps	£150	£
Curtains, carpets, rugs etc	£600	£
Other items		£
	Total	£

DINING ROOM	EXAMPLE NEW PRICE	YOUR ESTIMATE
Tables, chairs	£500	£
Pictures, clocks, ornaments, lamps	£100	£
Curtains, carpets, rugs etc	£400	£
China, glass and cutlery	£300	£
Sideboards, other furniture	£300	£
Other items		£
	Total	£

KITCHEN/UTILITY ROOM	EXAMPLE NEW PRICE	YOUR ESTIMATE
Washing machine, tumble dryer	£400	£
Dishwasher	£300	£
Refrigerator, freezer	£300	£
Cooker, microwave	£450	£
Table, chairs	£200	£
Crockery, cutlery, tools and utensils	£200	£
Electrical appliances	£250	£
Floor coverings, curtains	£250	£
Food, drink	£200	£
Other items		£
	Total	£

HALL, STAIRS, LANDING	EXAMPLE NEW PRICE	YOUR ESTIMATE
Furniture	£100	£
Blankets, towels and household linen	£250	£
Pictures, ornaments	£ 75	£
Curtains, carpets, rugs etc	£750	£
Other items		£
	Total	£

BATHROOM	EXAMPLE NEW PRICE	YOUR ESTIMATE
Bathroom furniture, cabinet etc	£ 75	£
Floor coverings, blinds	£100	£
Other items		£
	Total	£

MAIN BEDROOM	EXAMPLE NEW PRICE	YOUR ESTIMATE
Bed(s) and bedding	£300	£
Bedroom furniture	£750	£
Pictures, clocks, lamps, mirrors	£150	£
Curtains, carpets, rugs etc	£275	£
Other items		£
	Total	£

OTHER BEDROOMS	EXAMPLE NEW PRICE	YOUR ESTIMATE
Bed(s) and bedding	£350	£
Bedroom furniture	£650	£
Pictures, clocks, lamps, mirrors	£150	£
Curtains, carpets, rugs etc	£300	£
Other items		£
	Total	£

GARAGE/OUTBUILDINGS	EXAMPLE NEW PRICE	YOUR ESTIMATE
Garden tools	£100	£
DIY tools etc	£100	£
Lawnmower	£150	£
Garden furniture	£200	£
Other items		£
	Total	£

PERSONAL EFFECTS

Clothing (excluding furs) and all other personal articles (including toys, sports equipment and pedal cycles) worn used or carried other than valuables and money.	Husband's	£
	Wife's	£
	Children	£
	Other items	£
	Total	£

VALUABLES

Jewellery, watches, articles of gold, silver and other precious metals, furs, cameras, binoculars, pictures and other works of art and collections of stamps, coins and medals.	Husband's	£
	Wife's	£
	Children	£
	Other items	£
	Total	£

Money	Total	£

Now transfer all the totals to the grid below.

TOTALS	YOUR ESTIMATE
Sitting Room	£
Dining Room	£
Kitchen/Utility Room	£
Hall, Stairs, Landing	£
Bathroom	£
Main Bedroom	£
Other Bedrooms	£
Other Rooms	£
Garage/Outbuildings	£
SUB TOTAL	£
Personal effects	£
Valuables	£
Money	£
The value of your contents is . . .	**£**

THIS IS THE SUM FOR WHICH YOU SHOULD INSURE YOUR CONTENTS

Source: Guardian Royal Exchange.

48

fashioned indemnity cover which gives you a reduced pay-out depending on wear-and-tear as this is generally the type of cover included in the combined policies. However, it is possible if you are buying contents insurance separately to choose the level of cover most appropriate to your chequebook and needs. Table Eight explains the options, but a good specialist insurance broker should be able to help you through the minefield and find the best value for money cover for a home in your street.

About one in every four households has no insurance cover for their contents and if you fall ito this category it is time you reassessed your current situation. Many more people fail to increase the amount of cover each year to take account of both additional items and the rising costs of replacing the contents which have been insured.

Table Nine: Contents Insurance Update

Line A	Existing replacement value of general contents	£ _____
Line B	Valuables	£ _____
Line C	Updated replacement value of general contents	£ _____
Line D	Updated valuation of valuables	£ _____
Line E	Additional articles acquired over year	£ _____
Total new requirement	C+D+E	£ _____

There are no hard and fast rules on how to estimate the additional costs of replacing your existing contents, short of doing all the sums over again. However, if you simply adjust the figure to take account of inflation you should be in the right ball park. Remember that expensive items such as jewellery and furs will need to be listed separately and ideally you should keep the original receipt and have them valued regularly. If you do not want to pay for another professional

Table Eight   Cost of Contents Cover

| Type of of Policy | Cost per thousand pounds worth of cover in | | | Range of Cover |
	High Risk Area	Medium Risk Area	Low Risk Area	
Indemnity	£6.00–£10.00	£4.50– £8.00	£2.30– £3.00	Pays the current value of items after a deduction for wear and tear.
Indemnity plus some new-for-old	£6.50–£14.50	£4.50–£11.50	£2.40– £3.00	This policy will give you new-for-old cover on items until they are two to three years old. It offers indemnity cover for older items.
New-for-old	£7.50–£16.00	£3.30–£15.00	£2.50– £4.70	Pays the current replacement value of all items, except clothes and household linen.
New-for-old plus accidental damage	£8.90–£17.50	£4.60–£15.50	£4.20– £6.50	For an additional premium you can add accidental damage cover.
All risks–most items	£13.00–£18.00	£8.00–£12.00	£5.50– £7.50	A policy that offers you the opportunity of insuring some specified items, such as cameras, on an all risks basis. You could also add some accidental damage cover to this.
All risks–valuables, including jewellery	£25.00–£40.00	£12.00–£35.00	£7.50–£13.50	Every item is covered on an all risks basis.

Based on data in January 1987.

valuation, ring the shop where you purchased the item and find out the current price.

Extras

Apart from the basic range of policies you can add frills to suit your own tastes and requirements. For example, you may wish to have additional personal legal expense cover to protect you against the cost of litigation. A few policies automatically include this without charge, but if you are unhappy with the amount of cover, a specialist insurance broker will help.

There are a range of cases when it may be better to purchase cover for certain items separately by buying specialist policies. For example, if you collect antiques or own musical instruments or if your valuables add up to more than 5% of the value of your contents. In such cases, it may be worthwhile seeing whether there are specialist policies available, which although they may not be cheaper, may provide you with greater cover, e.g. in the case of instruments the policy would not only cover theft and damage, but also pay towards the hire of an alternative instrument. Also you may conclude that some of your valuables could be more safely stored and more cheaply insured if placed in the vault of a bank or specialist security company.

Cutting costs

As we have seen you may be able to save money by switching to a combined contents and building policy. There are also several other ways you can cut your costs without reducing the level of cover. These are:

- set up neighbourhood watch scheme. Some insurance companies will give a price discount of 2½% if you do this

- increase your home's security. Again this may entitle you to an extra discount

- if there is someone at home during the day and you have not made a claim for the past three years, then some companies will give you a discount.

- by asking a broker for a free estimate on the cost of purchasing the cover you require from various companies
- by putting some of your valuables in a bank vault or other secure place

Each insurance company sets its own price tariff and this is based on their experience in your area. This means one company might rate your home as a high risk and another as medium. Household insurance is one area where it really pays to seek professional advice – it will not cost you anything as the insurance company builds in the fees it would pay a broker into the overall cost of your policy.

Household insurance is not a very profitable area for insurance companies but it has become very competitive in recent years. Although companies want to charge the going rate to all customers they are not keen to lose their existing policyholders by penalising those who have not claimed for the general rise in crime. So an increasing number of companies are likely to introduce the equivalent of no-claims bonuses, common on car policies. If the company you are with does not do this automatically, you should try asking them for a discount if you have been a policyholder for many years and have never claimed.

You can find a specialist broker by writing to the British Insurance Brokers' Association, 14 Bevis Marks, London EC3A 7NT, enclosing a stamped addressed enveloped and requesting a list of companies who arrange household insurance in your area. Remember the cost of their fees is included in the policy, so you might as well benefit from their advice.

CHAPTER FOUR:
ON THE ROAD

In the twentieth century it is probably fair to say that man's best friend is not his dog but his car. Under the Road Traffic Act every motorist must have a minimum level of insurance cover which will pay out if you injure other people, known in the jargon as 'third parties'. Most people top this up with cover to protect the driver or potential drivers and the car itself in case of accident.

Picking the best motor policy is almost as hard as choosing a household contents policy even though you are only insuring one item not hundreds. The point to remember is that you need to work out clearly in advance just how much and what type of cover you require and make sure you spell out the details about both you, your car and the circumstances in which the car will be driven. Other key factors will be your home address, since the insurance company will feed this data into the computer when assessing the likelihood of your car being robbed and so set your policy costs accordingly and the number, age and experience of those who may be driving the car. Since on average people who own their own homes move about once every five years and those with families may wish to let their children drive, you can see that keeping your motor cover up to date should be high on your list of priorities.

Before picking a policy fill in Table One as it will help you define your needs and put at your fingertips the information you need to tell a broker or insurance company. The table has been compiled with the assistance of Legal and General Assurance Society.

Table One: Your Motoring Profile

Forenames ....

Surname ....

Address ....

....

County .... Post code....................

Date of birth ....

Give specific details of your business or occupation including part time work. (General answers such as 'manager' or 'director' are not acceptable.) ....

....

Address at which car is kept if different from above ....

....

Make of car ....

Model ....

Engine capacity ....

Year made ....

Registration mark ....

Seating capacity ....

Date of purchase ....

Estimated value ....

State type of car body (e.g. saloon, coupé, estate, sports car) ....

Has the car been adapted or modified from the maker's standard specification? If 'Yes' give details ....

....

....

Is the car owned by you? If 'No' give details ....

....

Is the car registered in your own name? If 'No' give details ....

....

Will the car normally be kept in a locked garage at night? ....

Do you currently own or have regular use of any other vehicle? If 'Yes' give details ....

Name of previous insurers ....

....

Do you currently qualify for a no-claim discount? ....

Has any insurer:

    Turned down your application ....

    Imposed special conditions ....

    Cancelled your policy ....

    Refused to renew your policy ....

The standard policy covers use for social, domestic and pleasure purposes and use by policyholder and his or her partner in connection with his/her business as stated excluding hiring, racing, competitions, rallies or trials, commercial travelling and use in connection with the motor trade.

Will the car be used for business purposes by any person other than yourself and your spouse? If 'Yes' give details

....

....

Will the car be used for hiring or for the carriage of passengers for hire or reward? If 'Yes' give details ....

....

Will the car be used for commercial travelling or in connection with the motor trade? ....

Will the car be used on any aerodrome or for the carriage of any substance of an explosive, inflammable, corrosive, toxic or otherwise dangerous nature?

If 'Yes' give details ....

....

....

Will the car be driven by:

    You alone ....

    You and your partner ....

    People over 30 years old ....

    Other, please specify ....

Who will be the main user of the car? ....

Give the following details about drivers who are to be covered by the policy:

Name ....

Age ....

Occupation (full-time) ....

Occupation (part-time) ....

Details of driving licence, i.e. type and length held ....

Details are required about the following for all potential drivers:

Accidents in the last four years ....
....

Claims in the last four years ....
....

Losses in the last four years ....
....

Convictions in the last four years ....
....

Any prosecutions pending ....
....

Any medical disabilities ....
....

Choosing your policy

By law drivers must purchase insurance which will pay out if they cause personal injury to third parties. This is known either as Road Traffic Act cover or 'third party only' cover. Then there is 'third party, fire and theft' which in addition to paying out in cases of personal injury will also provide cover if you damage someone else's property or if you suffer loss because the car is stolen or damaged by fire. The most extensive cover is known as comprehensive. This pays out in the same circumstances as third party, fire and theft but, subject to the individual policy details, gives you full protection if your car is damaged by other causes.

As with all types of insurance the greater the level of cover the greater the cost. Although as a general rule you should always purchase as much cover as you can afford when it comes to motor insurance you should match the cover to the car. If you or your children have an old banger then the cheaper third party, fire and theft may be sufficient, while the main family car should be protected by a fully comprehensive policy. If you would be devastated if your car was damaged you should try and find a comprehensive policy which includes loss of use. This will pay towards the hire of an alternative vehicle for a certain period of time.

Table Two shows the cost to a couple aged between thirty-five and forty-five of purchasing various types of motor insurance to cover a Cavalier 1.6GL less than four years old, assuming that they do not qualify for a no-claims bonus and that the car can be driven by anyone over the age of twenty-five years old. The figures have been supplied by Legal and General. For comparative purposes the illustrations are given for families living in Eastbourne and the centre of Stockport.

Table Two: Comparative Costs

Type of cover	Annual premium for car owner living in	
	Eastbourne	Central Stockport
Comprehensive	£410	£490
Third party, fire and theft	£182	£215
Third party only	£154	£182

Source: Legal and General, May 1987.

The above figures assume that the couple do not qualify for a no-claims bonus. Legal and General will reduce the charge of motor insurance cover by up to 60% if you have a good record of not claiming against your insurance policy. They operate a rising scale of discounts, starting with 30% if you have not claimed for one year and ending at 60% if you have not claimed for four years.

There are various other ways you can reduce costs. If you

choose a comprehensive policy you can volunteer to pay say the first portion of any claim yourself and this may cut your insurance cost by around 7%. Another way to achieve a substantial saving is to restrict the members of your household or friends who are permitted under the policy to drive the car. Table Three shows how it is possible to minimise your motor insurance costs. It is based on the same two families, living respectively in Eastbourne and Stockport, but this time assumes the cover is restricted to husband and wife and that they qualify for the full 60% no-claims bonus.

Table Three: Cutting The Costs

| Type of cover | Annual premium for car owner living in | |
	Eastbourne	Central Stockport
Comprehensive	£152.00	£176.80
Comprehensive with £50 excess	£136.80	£160.00
Third party, fire and theft	£65.20	£76.40
Third party only	£56.80	£65.20

Source: Legal and General, May 1987.

Table Four: Policies For The Over-sixties

| | Eastbourne | | Stockport | |
Type of cover	Over 60 but not retired	Over 60 and retired	Over 60 but not retired	Over 60 and retired
Comprehensive	£117.00	£108.23	£137.00	£126.73
Third party, fire and theft	£63.00	£58.28	£71.00	£65.68

Notes:
Insurance is for a group three car, i.e. Cavalier 1.6 GL aged less than four years old.
Cover is for husband and wife between the ages of sixty and seventy-five. The policy is written nett, i.e. the no claims discount does not apply.

Source: Legal and General, May 1987. For full details contact the insurance company direct or your regular insurance broker.

Even further reductions are available for those over sixty, especially if they are retired. Table Four indicates Legal and General's charges. These costs are net, i.e. it is not possible to reduce the cost by applying a no-claims discount to the fees quoted. There are certain restrictions apart from the age of the policyholder. The car must be a standard family car and used only for what is described as 'social, domestic and pleasure' purposes which includes trips to and from work.

Table Four: Annual Cost of Running Your Car

	Engine Capacity (cc)				
	Up to 1000	**1001 to 1500**	**1501 to 2000**	**2001 to 3000**	**3001 to 4500**
Standing Charges per annum (£)					
a. Car Licence	100.00	100.00	100.00	100.00	100.00
b. Insurance	356.60	402.50	484.90	750.00	1013.80
c. Depreciation	662.87	919.79	1135.87	2194.77	2946.50
d. Interest on Capital	424.24	588.67	726.96	1404.65	1885.76
e. Garage/Parking	208.00	208.00	208.00	208.00	208.00
f. Subscription	39.25	39.25	39.25	39.25	39.25
	1790.96	2258.21	2694.98	4696.67	6193.31
Running Cost per mile (in pence)					
g. Petrol*	4.350	4.971	5.800	7.909	8.700
h. Oil	0.388	0.388	0.413	0.456	0.745
i. Tyres	0.458	0.573	0.705	1.295	1.692
j. Servicing	0.736	0.736	0.736	0.961	1.434
k. Repairs & Replacements	4.418	4.677	5.466	8.270	10.278
Pence	10.350	11.345	13.120	18.891	22.849
*At £1.74 per gallon (38.3p per litre). For every penny more or less add or subtract	0.025	0.028	0.033	0.045	0.050
Total Cost Per Mile – based on 10,000 miles					
Standing Charges	17.910	22.582	26.950	46.967	61.933
Running Costs	10.350	11.345	13.120	18.891	22.849
Pence	28.260	33.927	40.070	65.858	84.782

Source: AA, April 1987.

Notes: This schedule is only intended as a guide. The figures quoted are average only and where possible members should make adjustments to suit their individual circumstances.

a. Car licence £100.00.
b. Insurance – average rates for a fully comprehensive policy. No allowance is made for no claim discount.
c. Depreciation – based on average car prices when new, a mileage of 10,000 per annum, and assuming an economical life of 80,000 miles or eight years. In the case of high annual mileage and secondhand vehicles the depreciation should be assessed individually.
d. Interest on capital – new car value is invested at 8% per annum. This element must be adjusted in the case of secondhand vehicles according to the prices paid.
e. Garage/parking £4.00 per week.
f. AA membership subscription including Relay.
g. Petrol £1.74 per gallon – *See note in table.
h. Engine oil – allowance is made for variable consumption throughout the car's life and the cost of replacement after oil changes.
i. Tyres – estimated tyre life of 30,000 miles.
j. Servicing – general servicing as recommended by the manufacturers. In the case of older motor cars servicing costs may be more.
k. Repairs and replacements – estimated on a basis of total cost of repairs, replacements and renovations over eight years or 80,000 miles at an average labour charge of £18.40 per hour, inclusive of VAT. However this figure can only be accurately assessed by the individual owner, as repair costs will vary even with identical models.

You must be resident in England, Scotland or Wales and have evidence of four years claim free driving. Finally, you must be in good health.

According to government figures on average we spend roughly 25% of our net earnings on transport, the third largest single item after housing and food. It therefore makes sense to ensure you are arranging your transport needs in the most cost effective manner. Most people have little or no idea how much it costs them to keep their car on the road each year and how much they could save by opting either for a different model or varying their means of transport. Table Four will help you work out the true cost of running your car.

One easy way to cut costs is to switch to a model which does not need so many gallons of petrol to the mile. Table Five gives some comparative information on this based on AA testing, which is a free service it offers its members.

Based on petrol at £1.74 per gallon the fuel costs of the VW Golf 1.6 Turbo Diesel are roughly 60% less than that of the Austin Metro 1.3 Auto over 10,000 miles.

Table Five: Oiling The Wheels

Model	Miles per Gallon	Cost of Driving 10,000 miles*
VW Golf 1.6 Turbo Diesel	53	£328.30
Vauxhall Astral 1.6 Diesel 4sp	51	£341.17
Austin Metro 1.0 City	43	£404.65
Vauxhall Astra 1.3 5sp	40½	£429.62
Austin Maestro 1.3 4sp	40	£435.00
VW Golf 1.6 GL 5sp	38½	£451.94
Seat Ibiza 1.5 GLX	38	£457.89
Austin Montego 1.6L 5sp	37	£470.27
Ford Escort 1.4 5sp	37	£470.27
Ford Sierra 1.6 5sp	35½	£490.14
Vauxhall Cavalier 1.6 5sp	35½	£490.14
Austin Metro 1.3 Auto	32½	£535.38

Source: AA, April 1987.

Note: Miles per gallon was based after testing the cars at a number of different speeds.

*Assuming petrol at £1.74 per gallon.

Although the tax benefits of company cars have been reduced by the Thatcher government in the 1987 Budget they still represent a perk well worth having.

Only company directors or those earning in excess of £8,500 are taxed on their company car. The tax is made up of two parts: a levy on the vehicle itself and the amount of petrol you are assumed to have used for non-business purposes. Three tables are used to assess the benefit of the car itself.

These cover:
- cars which cost up to £19,250 and have a stated cylinder capacity
- cars which cost up to £19,250 but do not have a cylinder capacity
- cars with an original market value of more than £19,250.

The Tables A to E show the value the Inland Revenue places on various categories of cars and the actual tax bill you would pay assuming you only pay basic rate tax at 27%. To work out your own tax bill you simply add the Inland Revenue's stated value of the benefit to your gross income and it is then subject to your rate of income tax on that slice, i.e. taxed at your highest rate of income tax.

You do not pay tax on petrol if your company gives you an allowance per business mile. However, if you are provided with petrol then this is taxed as a benefit. The tax levied is based on the recognised cylinder capacity, i.e. engine size unless this is not available, when the market value of the car is used instead. Again the cash equivalent of the perk is added to your gross income and taxed as part of your earnings. The tables show you the current scales.

Table A: Car Benefit – Cars with original market value up to £19,250 and having a cylinder capacity

Cylinder Capacity of Car in Cubic Centimetres	SCALE CHARGES		Tax Payable for 1988/89, (Assuming Basic-Rate Taxpayer and basic rate of 27p)	
	Age of Car at End of Relevant Year of Assessment		Age of Car at End of Relevant Year of Assessment	
	Under 4 Years	4 Years or More	Under 4 Years	4 Years or More
1400cc or less	580 (525)	380 (350)	£156.60	£102.60
1401cc – 2000cc	770 (700)	520 (470)	£207.90	£140.40
More than 2000cc	1210 (1100)	800 (725)	£326.70	£216.00

Table B: Car Benefit – Cars with original market value up to £19,250 and *not* having a cylinder capacity

Original Market Value of Car	SCALE CHARGES		Tax Payable for 1988/89, (Assuming Basic-Rate Taxpayer and basic rate of 27p)	
	Age of Car at End of Relevant Year of Assessment		Age of Car at End of Relevant Year of Assessment	
	Under 4 Years	4 Years or More	Under 4 Years	4 Years or More
Less than £6,000	580 (525)	380 (350)	£156.60	£102.60
£6,000 or more but less than £8,500	770 (700)	520 (470)	£207.90	£140.40
£8,500 or more but less than £19,250	1210 (1100)	800 (725)	£326.70	£216.00

Table C: Car Benefit – Cars with original market value more than £19,250.

Original Market Value of Car	SCALE CHARGES		Tax Payable for 1988/89, (Assuming Basic-Rate Taxpayer and basic rate of 27p)	
	Age of Car at End of Relevant Year of Assessment		Age of Car at End of Relevant Year of Assessment	
	Under 4 Years	4 Years or More	Under 4 Years	4 Years or More
£19,250 or more but not more than £29,000	1595 (1450)	1070 (900)	£430.65	£288.90
More than £29,000	2530 (2300)	1685 (1530)	£683.10	£454.95

Table D: Car Fuel Benefit – Cars with a recognised cylinder capacity

Cylinder Capacity of Car in Cubic Centimetres	Cash Equivalent	Tax Payable for 1988/89, (Assuming Basic-Rate Taxpayer and basic rate of 27p)
Up to 1400cc	480	£129.60
1401cc – 2000cc	600	£162.00
More than 2000cc	900	£243.00

Table E: Car Fuel Benefit – Cars not having a recognised cylinder capacity

Original Market Value of Car	Cash Equivalent	Tax Payable for 1988/89, (Assuming Basic-Rate Taxpayer and basic rate of 27p)
Less than £6,000	480	£129.60
£6,000 or more but less than £8,500	600	£162.00
£8,500 or more	900	£243.00

The number of miles you drive the company car in the tax year, i.e. April 6 through April 5 may also affect your tax bill. If you do 18,000 business miles or more in the relevant period then your tax charge on both the car itself and the fuel is halved. However, if the number of business miles you clock up falls to 2,500 or less or the car is a second company vehicle then your tax bill is increased by 50%.

If you have a car phone installed then that is treated as a separate perk and taxable as such, depending on the value the Inland Revenue places on it. You may also find your parking facilities are a taxable benefit if the company itself is charged a fee for providing them.

If driving to work is impractical you may be able to reduce your travel costs by getting your employer to help you finance the cost of your season ticket. Most large companies are prepared to give their employees an interest free loan to cover the annual cost of their season ticket. However, if you are a director or earn more than £8,500 then the benefit you enjoy is taxable, i.e. you pay income tax on the value of the interest you would have paid on the loan. So if you were lent £1,000 for a year and the normal interest charge would be £140 then this sum would be added to your earnings and taxed as income. In this case if you paid tax at the basic rate of 27% your bill would be £37.80.

CHAPTER FIVE:
HOME TRUTHS

For most people, buying their own homes has been the main way that families have accumulated wealth. Residential property prices in this country have risen dramatically. In 1970 the average cost of a home was a mere £5,000 but by 1986 the price tag had rises to £38,121, an increase of 662%. Over the same period the London stock market as measured by the FT All-Share Index had risen by 480% from 134.9 to 782.1.

What's more the tax position for UK residents wishing to buy their own home is extremely favourable. Whereas you invest money which has already been subject to tax once into shares and then see it taxed again, when you buy your home you receive tax relief on mortgage interest payments up to the statutory limit and gains from its subsequent sale are tax free.

So going back to 1970 let's assume you were given a cheque for £5,000 and used this to purchase your home outright. If the you sold the property at the end of 1986, assuming you received the average price of homes in this country for the sake of this example, then you would be sitting on a tax free gain of £33,121 minus legal costs and any estate agent's fees. On the other hand, you might have preferred to use the money to have a flutter on the stock market – in which case you would probably need the help of an accountant to work out your after tax return. There are two ways of earning money on shares, first an income in the form of dividends and second a capital gain if prices rise.

In this example we have assumed that the price of your

shares rose in line with the rise in the FT All Share Index over the same period. The index does not include any income so we have assumed your shares produced 5% gross per annum and have applied the average basic rate income over the period, 34.85%, to your stream of income. Finally, we have calculated your capital gains tax bill. Since March 31, 1982 gains on shares have been indexed and capital gains tax applies only to the indexed gain. In plain English this means you do not pay capital gains tax on rises in share prices which match the equivalent rise in the Retail Prices Index between that date and the time you sell. When working out your indexation allowance you have the choice of applying it either to the value of your shares on March 31, 1982 or their original cost. To maximise the value of the allowance to you you should always pick the higher share value.

Table One: After Tax Return on Property Versus Shares 1970-1986

	Property	Shares
Initial cost	£ 5,000	£ 5,000
Sales proceeds	£38,121	£24,000
Capital gain	£33,121	£19,000
Chargeable gain	Nil	£17,196
Capital Gains Tax bill	Nil	£ 3,268
Income	Nil	£10,900
Tax on income	Nil	£ 3,799
Total after tax gain	£33,121	£22,833

Notes:
1. The chargeable gain on the shares has been calculated as follows. The indexation allowance from March 31, 1982 to December 31,1982 is 0.254. This figure has then been applied to the price of the shares assuming they had risen in line with the FT All Share Index which stood at 326.59 on March 31, 1982.
2. The capital gains tax bill has been calculated on the assumption that the investor could make full use of the £6,300 tax free allowance for the tax year 1986-7.

As you can see from the example the tax system magnifies the relative superiority of property over shares as an investment medium during 1970 to 1986, even though that period included several years of booming share prices. In addition, given the availability of tax relief against your highest level of income tax on mortgage interest payments on loans of up to £30,000, property is clearly one of the best homes for your money.

Does that mean therefore that you should borrow up to the hilt to buy the most expensive property you can stretch to? In the second half of the seventies when the rate of inflation was often in double figures this made a great deal of sense. That is because you were paying back in pound notes which were worth less than you borrowed. If you then take into account the tax relief you received on mortgage interest payments you can see what a good deal you were getting.

Table Two: Average Rate of Mortgage Interest

	Gross	Net of standard rate tax
1970	8.58%	5.04%
1971	8.59%	5.30%
1972	8.26%	5.06%
1973	9.59%	6.71%
1974	11.05%	7.40%
1975	11.08%	7.20%
1976	11.06%	7.19%
1977	11.05%	7.29%
1978	9.55%	6.40%
1979	11.94%	8.35%
1980	14.92%	10.44%
1981	14.01%	9.80%
1982	13.30%	9.12%
1983	11.03%	7.72%
1984	11.84%	8.30%
1985	13.47%	9.42%
1986	11.85%	8.41%

Source: Building Societies Association Bulletin and Year Book. Tax rates used apply to the majority of the specified year and three months of the following year.

Nowadays, the cost of borrowing money is lower but so is inflation, so in fact the real cost of borrowing has actually risen. If inflation is running at 18% and the interest rate is 20%, the real cost is just 2%. However, if inflation is running at 5% and the interest rate is 12%, then the real cost of borrowing is a massive 7%.

So when deciding how much to borrow for your home you need to weigh up the real cost of such borrowings versus the potential benefits, which will of course depend on the ultimate sale price of the property. In this way you will see just how good or bad an investment your property really is.

Do not forget the actual sum you will be able to borrow will depend upon the lender's valuation of the property in question and your income. Roughly speaking most lenders will happily lend you the equivalent of 80% of the property's value subject to them being satisfied of your ability to repay. In judging your creditworthiness they will take into account your current income, assets and debts and your future prospects. Most lenders operate within the broad confines of certain guidelines laid down by their head office, which will reflect both the availability of mortgage funds and that group's experience of bad debts in the past. When home loan money is freely available you may be able to borrow up to three times your gross annual salary while in times of mortgage famine it may come down to one and three quarters. If applicable, your partner's or co-purchasers' salary will also be taken into account, although usually only one or one and a half times its value is added.

Loan options

So far we have just looked at a straightforward loan as a means of financing your house purchase, but in fact there are several options which you may wish to consider. When you arrange a home loan known as a 'repayment mortgage' you gradually repay the loan month by month. If you have taken on a £30,000, 25 year, repayment mortgage by year four you will have repaid around 15% and will only be paying

Table Three: Repayment versus Low-Cost Endowment

	Twenty-five year loan of:					
	£30,000		£40,000		£50,000	
	Repayment	Endowment	Repayment	Endowment	Repayment	Endowment
Monthly outlay	£231.68	£229.22	£387.08	£399.80	£483.64	£499.50
Average tax relief on interest	Payments made net	Payments made net	£ 58.85	£ 70.88	£ 62.41	£ 70.88
Average net outlay	£231.68	£229.21	£328.23	£328.92	£421.23	£428.62
Estimated surplus after repaying the mortgage	Nil	£14,409	Nil	£19,212	Nil	£ 24,015

Source: Abbey National Building Society, June 1987.

71

interest on the remainder. The alternative methods involve effectively borrowing the same £30,000 against the security of your home and an investment plan for say twenty-five years and only repaying the loan itself at the end of the term. So you agree to pay the interest on the whole loan for twenty-five years and contribute to an investment plan over the same time span. The theory being at the end of the twenty-five years not only will you own your home, which itself should have increased in value, but you will also have a tax-free lump sum from your investment plan.

The two main types of investment plan which can be used in this way at the moment are: endowment life assurance policies and personal pensions. In due course if the sums you are permitted to invest in personal equity plans are increased companies may offer these as part of a home loan package. Personal pensions are available to the self-employed and those who have what is called non-pensionable earnings, i.e. not participants in an occupational pension scheme. This rules out this option for the vast majority of employees at the moment, although after the rules on pensions are changed in January 1988 many more people will be permitted to buy personal pensions which can be used to support their application for mortgage funds.

Repayment versus endowment

So, to begin with we will look at the comparative merits of opting for a repayment mortgage versus a low cost endowment mortgage. Table Three has been compiled with the help of the Abbey National Building Society and is based on figures as at the end of June, 1987. The figures show the cost of borrowing £30,000, £40,000 and £50,000 for twenty-five years at an interest rate of 10.5% gross assuming the borrower was a man aged thirty. The estimated surplus after the mortgage has been repaid is based on the assumption that the life assurance company managing the endowment policy, in this case Standard Life, produced an annual return of 10.75%. We have added the cost of a mortgage protection policy to the charges for a repayment mortgage which would ensure that if the borrower died the loan would be repaid in full. This cover is included in the endowment policy and does not need to be purchased separately. Since under current rules tax relief is only available on interest payments for mortgages up to £30,000 you will notice for the two larger sums there is a difference between the gross monthly outlay and the net. For the £30,000 loan the payments are made net of tax relief. We have assumed the borrower pays tax at 27%

Apart from the financial considerations there are also psychological factors to take into account. Many people like to feel that they are gradually working towards owning their own home and the falling size of their outstanding mortgage gives them some comfort. Others worry about the actual return the life assurance company will clock up, whether it will be sufficient to pay off the mortgage and what in terms of spending power the seemingly large cash surplus will mean to them in twenty-five years.

Pension mortgages

Pension mortgages have become increasingly popular ever since the government withdrew life assurance premium relief, a concession which boosted the value of your life assurance premiums. There are two tax advantages in using your pension, firstly your payments attract tax relief and secondly

Table Four: Cost of Pension Mortgages

	£30,000	£40,000	£50,000
Gross monthly outlay	£350.43	£467.21	£584.00
Net monthly outlay	£255.82	£364.70	£473.57
Estimated cash surplus after repaying the mortgage	£ 11,077	£ 14,764	£ 18,451
Estimated pension per annum	£ 12,973	£ 17,297	£ 21,621

Source: Abbey National Building Society, June 1987.

your money can grow tax free when invested. Table Four shows the cost of arranging a pension mortgage to cover home loans of £30,000, £40,000 and £50,000. Again we have assumed the borrower is a man aged thirty, paying tax at 27% and the mortgage rate of 10.5% gross. The retirement age has been set at fifty-five years and for comparative purposes we have assumed an annual return on the pension of 13%.

What you have to weigh up here is whether the additional sum is worth paying in terms of the benefit you receive, remembering that the true value of your ultimate lump sum will depend upon the cost of living in the future and that you cannot draw your pension until you have reached the retirement age stated in your policy. Much depends, of course, on the actual investment performance of your particular plan and this can vary dramatically from company to company as well as reflecting stock market conditions over the time. There may also be changes in the tax rules which affect the proportion of your pension you can draw as a tax-free lump sum rather than as taxed income.

As interest rates come down the relative merits of the various options alter. In broad terms if interest rates are low and the economy is booming, usually this is reflected in good returns on the stock market which then means an investment linked mortgage makes a great deal of sense. If interest rates are high, the economy sluggish and the stock market dragging its feet then a straightforward repayment loan comes into its own.

Remember that if you opt for an insurance plan you should regard this as a long term commitment. If cash gets short and you can no longer afford the premiums within the first five years then you will get a very poor return, sometimes less than the value of the money you invested.

On the first rung

As you can see there are sound financial reasons why you should strongly consider buying your own home. However, for many more people the choice is really taken out of their hands. Successive governments have introduced legislation which has increased tenants rights to such a degree that many would-be landlords have simply given up the idea. As a result we have a small and shrinking rented sector increasingly geared to short term lets and accommodation for foreigners. Although there appears to be the possibility of some change in the law and possibly the tax system to encourage the rebirth of the private rented sector this will inevitably take several years to materialise. In the meantime many young people are struggling to clamber up the first rung of home ownership.

If you fall into this category, the main issue you probably face is not about whether to invest more or less in your home but how to achieve home ownership given the current level of your income and wealth. Apart from the cost of the property you will need cash for furniture, moving expenses and to pay the various professionals involved, i.e. solicitor, surveyor etc. Table Five lists the items you will need to pay for, over and above the cost of the loan itself.

You then have two tasks: how to finance the home purchase and how to fund the additional and connected expenses. These can either be tackled separately or together. First let us look at the home loan situation. The government runs a home loan scheme for first time buyers who have saved regularly with their bank or building society. When you open your savings account tell the bank or building society you wish to participate and they will give you the appropriate form to complete. You need to keep at least £300 in your account for a full year. The more cash you accumulate, the more you benefit. The maximum interest free loan at present is £600 with up to £100 as a cash bonus. To prevent the scheme being abused the money given is only available to people buying relatively inexpensive homes. The government produces a list of qualifying price ceilings in various regions of the country. Table Six reproduces the list and as you see the figures for London and the South East are pretty low, where a converted cupboard in Knightsbridge went on sale in Spring 1987 for £35,000.

Table Five: Estimated Cost of Purchasing a Property

	Price of property:		
	£20,000 **£**	**£35,000** **£**	**£60,000** **£**
Building society valuation fee	57	74	86
Structural survey	202	233	293
Solicitor's fee	230	403	690
Building society solicitor's fee	77	87	88
Stamp duty	nil	350	600
lless – Searches	16	16	16
less – Land Registry fees	48	80	145
TOTAL	£630	£1,243	£1,918

NB. As at October 1, 1986. Assumes property is registered and solicitor's fees are equivalent to 1% plus VAT. Figures rounded to nearest pound.

How else can you reduce your borrowing cost? One option would be to choose what is called a low start mortgage. These are tailored to people on low incomes but who can anticipate a rising income in the years to come. There are various ways of structuring low start mortgages, sometimes you do not pay the full whack of interest charge in the first few years with the balance being rolled up and added to the capital. This means in effect your mortgage is getting bigger for the first few years and you will end up paying interest on interest. In other schemes you simply pay a lower rate of interest in the first few years and a higher rate to compensate later on.

First time buyers, especially in London and the South East, may even find these types of schemes too onerous. For them the answer could be what is called shared ownership, literally a half way house between renting and buying. The schemes are run by the Housing Corporation and housing associations. The property you wish to buy is first valued by a qualified valuer and then you can buy as little as 25% of the equity and rent the rest. In due course you can gradually buy more

Table Six: Home Loan Scheme

	As from 27.3.87 £	As from 25.9.86 £
ENGLAND **Northern Region:** Counties of Cleveland, Durham, Northumberland and Tyne and Wear	25,500	(22,100)
Yorkshire and Humberside Region: Counties of Humberside, North Yorkshire, South Yorkshire and West Yorkshire	24,800	(22,800)
East Midlands Region: Counties of Derbyshire, Leicestershire, Lincolnshire, Northamptonshire and Nottinghamshire	27,400	(24,200)
East Anglia Region: Counties of Cambridgeshire, Norfolk and Suffolk	34,600	(30,200)
South East Region: (London) County of Greater London	55,400	(45,700)
Rest of South East: Counties of Bedfordshire, Berkshire, Buckinghamshire, East Sussex, Essex, Hampshire, Hertfordshire, Isle of Wight, Kent, Oxfordshire, Surrey and West Sussex	44,600	(37,900)
South West Region: Counties of Avon, Cornwall, Devon, Dorset, Gloucestershire, Somerset and Wiltshire and the Isles of Scillly	35,600	(30,700)
West Midlands Region: Counties of Hereford and Worcester, Shropshire, Staffordshire, Warwickshire and West Midlands	26,900	(23,800)
North West Region: Counties of Cheshire, Cumbria, Greater Manchester, Lancashire and Merseyside	26,100	(23,600)
WALES	26,700	(24,100)
SCOTLAND	29,800	(27,500)

and more of the property until you own it outright. Details are available from regional offices of the Housing Corporation who will also be able to provide you with information on those housing associations offering the scheme in your area.

You will also have to find the cash for furniture, moving and those first few month's bills. Many building societies have taken advantage of their new freedom to introduce unsecured loans but these are not always cheaper than similar loans from a bank. Remember the key figure is the true rate of interest, known as the annual percentage rate (APR) which gives you the cost of borrowing over one year including any administrative charges.

You may be tempted to choose a package deal from a builder which includes a mortgage, legal fees and a fully furnished flat or house. The main advantage of such a deal is that you receive tax relief on your mortgage so are effectively borrowing money for consumer goods at a much cheaper rate than if you walked into a bank or building society. The main disadvantage is that the value of the package is likely to decrease over the first few years unless property prices in the area rise rapidly. That is because the next buyer will not want to pay very much for your by then old furniture and fittings. Indeed in some cases where large estates have been built people have found it difficult to sell their homes as quickly as they would have wished.

Home improvements

Moving home costs you around 5% of the price of the property you are purchasing plus often a lot of hassle and even some heartache. After a period of about a decade of sustained house price rises throughout most of the country the price offered for your current home might surprise you until you try to buy a replacement. Most of us buy larger and more expensive homes roughly every five years and go on trading up until retirement.

As we have seen our homes are one of our best investments

but often having forked out substantial sums for the initial purchase we tend to be rather mean on its upkeep. According to the Building Societies Association research we tend to spend our money on the wrong things, lavishing our hard earned cash on stone cladding and replacement glazing rather than a new roof or damp course.

Table Seven shows you which home improvements will add to the value of your property and which will not. Remember there is no point building a palace in a run-down area. The old estate agency's motto which should be remembered when buying or selling property is 'location, location, location'. Also take into account the likely preferences of the potential new owners.

Table Seven: Home Improvements

Type of Improvement	Estimated Cost	Benefits
Central heating	£3,000-£4,000	Will almost certainly add to the value of your home and is one of the most cost-effective improvements you can make. Overall heating bills may go up depending on what your heating arrangements are now but in terms of the amount of heating you get for your money central heating is the most efficient way of doing it.
Insulation: a) roof	£80-£100 plus labour (local authority grant of up to £95 available)	Will cut down heating bills dramatically and will certainly pay for itself within a year or two. If you get a grant to install or to up your insulation the cost can be negligible.
b) cavity walls	£250-£600	Will pay for itself in reduced heating bills within a few years. May add to value of house.

c) double glazing	£6,000 upwards	Probably not worthwhile if your windows are already in good condition. If they need replacing then the additional cost of double glazing will be partially recouped from lower bills. May contribute to an increase in the value of your house. Figures quoted are for a DIY secondary glazing system to a full replacement window installation.
d) Secondary glazing	£50-£500	Cost per widow depending on size and whether it is a professional job or DIY.
Kitchen refit	£2,000 upwards	May contribute to an increase in the value of your house. Will almost certainly increase its selling potential. However, it is easy to overspend and buyers may have different ideas about their ideal kitchen.
Conversions and extensions:		
a) pre-fab conservatory	£1,000 upwards	In general a brick and block built extension is likely to increase the value of your house while a prefabricated extension will not.
b) built exension	£5,000 upwards	

As at January, 1987.

You can enjoy tax relief on loans for home improvements provided it, together with your existing mortgage, is not above the statutory limit. The list below gives you some idea of what qualifies:

- Home extensions and loft conversions.

- Central and solar heating installation (excluding portable radiators and night storage radiators not fixed to a permanent spur outlet). The cost of replacing one form of heating with another for example changing from oil to gas central heating, is included.

- Installation of double-glazing even though it is in a detachable form. Replacement of windows or doors generally is included.

- Insulation of roof or walls.
- Installation of bathrooms and other similar plumbing.
- Kitchen and bedroom units (for example sink units) which are affixed to and become part of the building. In practice a range of matching units may be treated as qualifying as a whole even though only some of them qualify (but always excluding cookers, refrigerators and similar appliances).
- Connection to main drainage.
- Erection and cost of garages, garden sheds, greenhouses, patios and fences.
- Recovering or reconstructing a roof.
- Construction or landscaping of gardens.
- Construction of swimming pools.
- Reconstruction of property, e.g. conversion into flats.
- Underpinning a house.
- Rebuilding a facade.
- Insertion or renewal of damp-proof course. Dry and wet rot treatment.
- Replacement of electrical installations.
- Extensive repointing, pebble-dashing, texture coating or stone cladding (but excluding painting).
- Installation of fire or burglar alarms.
- Installation of water softening equipment forming a permanent part of the plumbing system.
- Construction of driveways and paths.
- Extensive replacement of guttering.

Perhaps the cheapest way of both adding value to your home and enjoying an immediate benefit from the investment is by making it more secure. Your local Crime Prevention Officer will help you decide what needs to be done and as we have seen in the chapter on insurance you may be able to either lower your insurance costs as a result or at least prevent them rising steeply.

81

Tables Eight and Nine give you some indication of the current cost and you can use Table Nine to go round your home and work out the cost of what needs doing. If you wish to install a burglar alarm most insurance companies recommend you hire a member of the National Supervisory Council of Intruder Alarms.

Table Eight: Securing Your Doors

TYPE OF SECURITY	HIGH £	MEDIUM £	ECONOMY £
A1 5-lever mortise deadlock BS 3621	19.00		
A2 5-lever mortise deadlock		11.50	11.50
B Door chain/door limiter	3.50	3.50	3.50
C Door viewer	3.50	3.50	
D Door hinge bolts (pair)	6.00		
E Security bolts (pair)	6.00		
Total DIY cost	38.00	18.50	15.00
Estimated fitting cost*	27.00	16.50	14.00
Total fitted price	65.00	35.00	29.00

*These costs may vary.

Source: Home Office Standing Conference on Crime Prevention leaflet.

Table Nine: Securing Your Windows

TYPE OF SECURITY		HIGH £	MEDIUM £	ECONOMY £
SASH WINDOWS	A Push to lock	5.00		
	B Quick fit		4.25	
	C Dual screws			1.60
WOOD HINGED WINDOWS	D Snap action	4.70		
	E Quick fit		3.75	
	F Easy fit			1.70
METAL HINGED WINDOWS	G Turn catch lock	6.50		
	H Quick fit		4.25	
	I Handle lock			2.90
Average DIY cost for 8 windows		44.00	35.00	16.00
Estimated fitting cost*		40.00	35.00	20.00
Total fitted price		84.00	70.00	36.00

NB: On poorly fitting and larger windows two locks should be fitted.
Source: Home Office Standing Conference on Crime Prevention leaflet.

Table Ten: Securing Your Home

(a) Flat £

Front door . . . . _____

Back door . . . . _____

Kichen window . . . . _____

Bathroom window(s) . . . . _____

Living room window . . . . _____

Bedroom window(s) . . . . _____

Dining room window . . . . _____

Other windows . . . . _____

Balcony . . . . _____

Alarm system . . . . _____

Total . . . . **_____**

(b) House £

Front door . . . . _____

Back door . . . . _____

Downstairs windows . . . . _____

Upstairs windows . . . . _____

Garage . . . . _____

Outbuildings . . . . _____

Garden . . . . _____

Alarm system . . . . _____

Total . . . . **_____**

CHAPTER SIX:
CASH FLOW

In any one year the average family handles about as much cash as the average small business person. If you talk to any businessmen they will regale you with stories about the importance of managing the company's cash flow properly especially when they are expanding. Many families, particularly those with children, are in a similar situation but they tend to let the habits of a lifetime dictate their financial affairs.

Cash multiplier

The first thing is to make sure you are paying the lowest possible sum for your personal banking, while earning the highest possible after tax interest on any cash balances. Table One shows you the comparative cost of running various types of bank account as at May 5, 1987, some of which pay interest on current account balances.

Accounts which pay interest on your savings are clear winners, but even so the difference is quite staggering. In this example, the best deal would be the Save & Prosper/ Robert Fleming High Interest Account where you would receive £56.30 over the year and the worst is the Royal Bank of Scotland where a charge of £55.44p would be levied.

Of course the cheapest option will depend upon your individual circumstances, i.e. balance in account, number of times you go overdrawn and how many transactions you perform. This is likely to change over time, which underlines the point about the need to alter your savings and investment habits as your life progresses. However, it also emphasises

Table One: Comparative Banking Costs

Rank	Bank	Interest credited (£)	Charge (£)	Net addition (Charge) to account over 12 months (£)
1.	Save & Prosper/ Robert Fleming & Co. Classic High Interest Bank Account	56.30	0.00	56.30
2.	Save & Prosper/ Robert Fleming & Co. Premier High Interest Bank Account	62.50	(24.00)	38.50
3.	Co-op Bank Cheque & Save account	50.34	(27.09)	23.25
4=	Barclays	0.00	0.00	0.00
4=	Lloyds	0.00	0.00	0.00
4=	NatWest	0.00	0.00	0.00
4=	TSB	0.00	0.00	0.00
8.	Alliance & Leicester Banksave Account	37.38	(39.00)	(1.62)
9.	Allied Dunbar Master Aaccount	22.50	(52.80)	(30.30)
10.	Bank of Scotland	0.00	(40.80)	(40.80)
11.	Yorkshire Bank	0.00	(49.44)	(49.44)
12.	TSB (Scotland)	0.00	(49.80)	(49.80)
13.	Clydesdale Bank	0.00	(50.40)	(50.40)
14.	Midland Bank	0.00	(52.60)	(52.60)
15.	Royal Bank of Scotland	0.00	(55.44)	(55.44)

Notes: The above table assumes an average balance of £1,000 and the following transactions per month:

- eight cheques
- two standing orders
- one direct debit
- two ATM withdrawals
- one automated credit
- one manual credit.

It also assumes that the account goes overdrawn once per quarter. The figures shown for 'interest credited' are based on a projection of interest rates as at 5.5.87, which may vary. The figures shown for bank charges are exclusive of any overdraft interest.

the importance of planning your banking services as part of your overall financial strategy.

Credit lines

It is not just a matter of maximising the return on your cash, but having the money free and available as and when you need it. There's no point feeling smug about earning say 6% net of basic rate tax on your cash in a high interest account if at the same time you are paying out 38% per annum to a store on your credit card borrowings. Of course it makes sense to take advantage of any offers of free credit. This includes using your credit cards to the maximum advantage since they can give you up to fifty-five days free credit. Providing you are not the sort of person who goes on wild shopping sprees the moment they spot a piece of plastic then using several of these cards, which are issued free by the banks, can help you cut down your borrowing costs if you plan your purchases to make the most of the gap between the date you buy the goods and the date you are billed.

For example, if you assume the cost of borrowing money is 13% per annum then the value of your fifty-five days free credit period is £1.96 per £100 and if you enjoyed a twenty-five days free credit period the value would be 89p per £100.

You can choose the cheapest form of credit by comparing what is called the annual percentage rate, which show the true rate of interest after taking into account any administrative costs. However, this does put credit cards in a rather poor light as no allowance is made for the fact you get up to fifty-five days free credit. This means for short term borrowings credit cards and even some store cards actually work out cheaper than bank overdrafts, especially when you take into account those dreaded bank charges which you will start to clock up once you go into the red. Table Two shows you the relative costs, taking into account bank charges, of borrowing £500 for one, two and three months. The comparisons will alter as interest rates fluctuate and the cost of bank charges changes. In this example we have taken an

Table Two: Comparative Costs of Short-Term Borrowing

£500 borrowed for:	1 month		
	Interest paid	Account charges	Approx. APR
Bank overdraft	£5.42	£14.31	58.2%
Credit card	£8.75	—	23.1%

£500 borrowed for:	2 months		
	Interest paid	Account charges	Approx. APR
Bank overdraft	£10.84	£14.31	34.0%
Credit card	£17.50	—	23.1%

£500 borrowed for:	3 months		
	Interest paid	Account charges	Approx. APR
Bank overdraft	£16.26	£14.31	26.8%
Credit card	£26.25	—	23.1%

Notes:
1. Overdraft interest at 13% with quarterly charging period
2. Account charges cover: eight cheques, two standing orders, one direct debit and two cash dispenser withdrawals per month.
3. Interest rate on credit card is 1.75% per month.

Table Three: Credit Ready Reckoner

	Minimum	Maximum	Time to repay	Interest rate % APR
Flexible credit				
Overdrafts				
i Arranged	None	What bank manager allows	As agreed	12.5.-16.5
ii Not arranged	None	" "	Depends on bank manager	Up to 25.0
Credit cards	None	Your credit	Indefinite	Up to 23.8
Gold cards:				
i Overdrafts	None	£7,500-£10,000	Indefinite	Around 13.0
ii Spending	None	None	Two weeks after statement date	Up to 20.0
Revolving credit				
i Banks	£180-£300	18-30 times monthly	Indefinite	Around 20.0
ii Shops	£90-£240	" "	Indefinite	30.0-35.0
Bank budget accounts	None	None	One year	£10-15 plus overdraft interest (around 20%, cheque and standing order charges

Table Three continued:

	Minimum	Maximum	Time to repay	Interest rate % APR
Planned credit				
Personal loans				
i Bank	£300-£500	£5,000-£7,500	One to three years (five for home improvements)	Around 20.0
ii Finance Company	£200	£10,000	One to five years	Around 32.0
Credit sale	Depends on retailer	Depends on retailer	Usually three years	Around 23.0
Insurance company				
i Credit plan	£30-£50	Total premiums 80-90% of surrender value	5-12 months Term of policy	6.0-14.0 11.5-13.0
ii Policy loan	£100-£250	Value of policy or 15 times yearly premium	Term of policy	12.5-16.5 plus setting up costs
ii Loanback	£15,001			

*Assumes bank base rates are 10 per cent.

90

overdraft rate of 13% flat and an interest rate on credit card borrowing of 1.75% per month. We have assumed relatively few transactions per account in the month: eight cheques, two standing orders, one direct debit and two cash dispenser withdrawals plus a standard quarterly charging period.

Getting over the humps

What can you do if you are suddenly hit by a cash crisis? Ideally you do not want to disturb any financial planning arrangements you have already made. You need to take a cool look at your situation and work out how much you'll need over what period of time. For short term borrowings on a fairly small scale as Table Three shows asking your insurance company for a loan against the security of your policy can prove a very cost effective option.

For longer term crises unlocking some of the value you have built up in your home by either extending the size of your mortgage or taking out a second mortgage may be the most tax efficient answer. Table Four shows you the comparative costs:

Table Four: Unlocking Your Savings

Route	APR%
Extending your mortgage	11.7+possible arrangement fee
Remortgaging your home	11.7+substantial fees
Loan against insurance policy	11.5-13+arrangement fee
Loanback of personal pension contribution	12.5-16.5+arrangement fee
Personal loan	20.6% (including arrangement fee)

Source: Save & Prosper Group.

Notes: Based on comparative costs in May 1987 of borrowing a sum in the order of £5,000. Arrangement fees will vary from lender to lender.

Remember you qualify for tax relief on the interest payments of home loans up to £30,000 which can reduce the net cost of adopting the route to extend your mortgage substantially. For many people the surprising statistic here is the relatively costly personal loan. This is partly because it is an unsecured loan, unlike your mortgage, and partly because the banks have traditionally been in the position of setting the market rates rather than responding to competition. With building societies entering the field of unsecured loans and greater competition across the board for your business we could see rates being reduced.

From time to time you may see adverts in the paper which promise to reduce the cost of financing your debts at a stroke and give you what is called 'free life assurance cover'. In fact, this is just an endowment-linked mortgage policy. This is a very inflexible option as if you stop paying premiums within the first five years you will get a very poor return on your money.

Red light

With an increasing number of companies urging you to take credit it is not surprising that more and more families are getting into debt. The warning signals are:

- your overdraft is growing each month
- you are taking out more and more expensive loans to pay off the interest on existing ones
- you are refused credit by your own bank

In this case, you need to engineer a breathing space. If you have a mortgage talk to the lender and see if you can reduce your monthly payments by extending the life of the mortgage. This may not be possible if you have an endowment mortgage, in which case you may need to switch to the lower cost option of a repayment mortgage. Contact the various companies who you owe money to, explain the position and work out how much you can afford to pay each one month. It's best to pay each company little and often, rather than pay off one and leave the rest waiting.

Most of the high street banks provide free checklists to help you monitor your expenditure and if accurately filled in they should help you highlight your own particular spending problems. Barclays Bank's breakdown is shown to give you some idea of how to keep tabs on your household bills.

These should be used in conjunction with the monthly cash flow sheet. It is a sad fact of life that bills, like many sorrows, tend to come in three's . . . if not four's or five's. Most utilities, such as gas, telephone and electricity tend to bill you quarterly, although you may be able to arrange for them to do so monthly. Most banks also run budget accounts which pay interest while you are in credit and allow you to borrow automatically a certain multiple of your monthly savings at a rate of interest less than their personal loan rates. This can be a cheaper option than going overdrawn and clocking up bank charges.

Table Five: Monthly Expenditure

EXPENDITURE	Annual	Quarterly	Monthly/ 4 Weekly	Weekly Equivalent
Mortgage/Rent				
Rates & Water Rate				
Property Maintenance				
House Contents & Bldgs Insce				
Life insurance				
Other Insurance (excl. car)				
Credit Card Repayments				
H.P. Commitments				
Personal Loan Repayments				
Heating (solid fuel/gas/oil)				
Electricity				
Gas				
Telephone				
Car Expenses*				
TV				
School Expenses*				
Fares/Season Ticket				
Clothing/Shoes				
Housekeeping*				
Club/Society Subscriptions				
Newspaper/Mag Subscriptions				
Savings/Investments				
Holiday Expenses*				
Presents*				
Pocket Money				
Other Expenses				
Total Estimated Expenditure	£	£	£	£

*See Expenditure Breakdown Sheet for detailed costs.

Table Six: Expenditure Breakdown

(Use in conjunction with Monthly Expenditure sheet.)

	Annual	Quarterly	Monthly/ 4 Weekly	Weekly Equivalent
Car Expenses Petrol				
Oil				
Maintenance				
Road Fund				
Insurance				
Replacement Fund				
Total				
School Expenses Uniforms				
Sports Equipment				
Subscriptions				
School Meals				
Fees				
Books				
Total				
Housekeeping Freezer				
Other Groceries, etc.				
Petfoods				
Total				
Presents Christmas				
Birthdays				
Total				
Holidays Deposit/Insurance				
Balance				
Trav. Cheques & Currency				
Total				

Table Seven: Cash Flow Month-by-month

MONTH-BY-MONTH	1	2	3	4	5	6	7
Balance from last month () ADD Income							
Monthly Expenditure ADD Quarterly } Annual } Items due this month							
Total Expenditure 'B'							
A — B = Balance to next month (±)							

MONTH-BY-MONTH	8	9	10	11	12	13	
Balance from last month (±) ADD Income							
Total Available 'A'							
Monthly Expenditure Add Quarterly } Annual } Items due this month							
Total Expenditure 'B'							
A — B = Balance to next month (±)							

How much is needed each month to meet your expenditure? Simply carry forward the monthly figure calculated on the monthly expenditure page and add the annual and quarterly figures.

Useful free leaflets

No Credit? Published by the Office of Fair Trading. This explains your rights to know what credit reference agencies are saying about you and how to get wrong information corrected.

Shop Around For Credit. Published by the Office of Fair Trading. A sixteen page booklet which explains the various types of credit available and gives helpful hints for potential borrowers.

The True Cost of Credit. Published by the Office of Fair Trading. This explains how to work out the actual cost of the loan and how to compare the charges of various different types of credit.

Debt: A Survival Guide. Published by the Office of Fair Trading.

CHAPTER SEVEN:
SAVE AS YOU EARN

One of the best types of insurance against those inevitable cash crises is a savings safety cushion. The sooner you start, the better. There is a wide range of regular savings plans on the market which cater for the various needs of those with upwards of £20 a month to save. Before you plunge in at the deep end fill in the savings planner, Table One.

By filling in this table you will be able to narrow down your choice. What you are looking for is the savings plan which will give you the highest return after tax while meeting your needs to get access to your money and your attitude to risk. Generally speaking the longer you can tie up your money and the greater the degree of risk you are prepared to take the higher the level of return, although some very speculative investments are very short term and can leave you even worse off than when you started. So steer clear of plans which promise instant fortunes, all too often the only person making the quick killing is the company selling the plan.

Making your choice

Each type of investment has been rated for risk. A five star is relatively low risk and applies to savings where your capital is returned to you in full and you earn interest. A four star provides almost the same degree of security except if you need to withdraw the cash before a specified date. A three star involves a degree of risk which is normally easy to define as it relates to changes in interest rates in the economy and only marginally to investors' sentiment. A two star involves the possibility of losing your capital but gives you the potential

Table One: Savings Planner

	£ Amount
1. Objective of saving e.g. Daughter's wedding Lifetime holiday Mortgage deposit New car Retirement nest-egg Other	
2. Time scale for saving e.g. Short-term – up to five years Medium-term – five to ten years Long-term – over ten years	
3. Accessibility e.g. Immediate At specified date Long-term	
4. Attitude to risk e.g. Low Moderate Speculative	
5. Tax position e.g. Now Anticipated over lifetime of savings plan Anticipated at end of savings plan	
6. Savings target	£
7. Current savings provision	£
8. SHORTFALL	£

for growth and a higher income. A one star is only for the brave – or foolhardy – and puts your money in a high risk situation. Table Two shows the star rating.

Table Two: Risk Rating

Investment	Capital at risk	Growth potential	Rating
Deposit account	No	Yes	★★★★★
National Savings	No	No	★★★★★
Government securities	Yes	Yes	★★★★
Corporate bonds	Yes	Yes	★★★
Ordinary shares	Yes	Yes	★★
Property	Yes	Yes	★★
Commodities	Yes	Yes	★
Futures	Yes	Yes	★
Options	Yes	Yes	★

● Deposit account

An account with a bank or building society on which you earn interest. They range from instant access account where you can withdraw your money straight away without loss of interest up to accounts where your money is tucked away for three, even five years. The interest is paid net of basic rate tax and higher rate taxpayers have to pay an additional tax charge when they fill in their tax return. Non-taxpayers cannot reclaim the interest. There is also a one month notice account run by National Savings which pays interest gross and is therefore more suitable for non-taxpayers. This is called the Investment Account.

● National Savings

This is an offshoot of the Treasury, although its products are sold over the post office counter. Its task is to raise cash for the government by selling products to the public. These include income bonds, deposit bonds and five year savings certificates. The tax treatment varies from product to product but none of the investments puts your capital at risk.

- Government securities

These are fixed rate stocks issued and guaranteed by the UK government. They are issued in units of £100 and in most cases the government agrees to repay each buyer £100 at or by a *specific date* in the future and in the meantime pay a stated rate of interest. So for example a stock called Treasury 10% 2000 would pay £10 a year income and holders would be repaid £100 per unit in the year 2000. If you buy the units for £100 and hold onto them until the year 2000 there is no risk to your capital. However the price of the units tend to fluctuate with interest rates. So if interest rates fall, people will start buying the gilt because a 10% income will look attractive. This will push up the price above £100, giving a built in capital loss for those who hold the stock until maturity. There is no tax on any capital gains while the income is taxable at your rate of income tax.

- Corporate bonds

These are fixed rate stocks issued by companies and are similar in most respects to government securities, except gains are liable to capital gains tax. They usually pay a higher rate of interest than government stock to reflect the slightly higher risk. That is because you are relying on the financial resources of the company to repay you at a particular date.

- Ordinary shares

These are shares in companies which entitle you to share a proportion of the company's earnings and assets after any prior claims have been settled. Your return is usually composed of an income via dividend payments twice a year and if the share price rises you will have a capital gain. There are no guarantees as to the future price movements of shares and if the company goes bust, you could find them worth just a few pence in the pound. Your dividends are paid net of basic rate tax, but this can be reclaimed by non taxpayers while higher rate taxpayers will have an additional bill. Any gains are liable to capital gains tax.

102

- Futures

These are contracts traded on recognised markets across the world whereby you agree to purchase a certain amount of a certain commodity for a stated price at a date in the future. The commodity could be coffee, chocolate or interest rates, strange as that sounds. You only need to make a small down payment, often equally to 20% of the contract. It is a very risky investment as you will only make a profit if the commodity rises in price and you can sell on your contract to someone who wishes to purchase at the stated price. If this does not happen by the time the contract falls due you have to cough up the remaining sum, say 80%. So if things go wrong you can lose more money than you originally staked. The tax treatment is not very favourable as gains are treated as earned income and taxed at your highest band.

- Options

The right to buy or sell a share at a given price within a given period. The price of the option tends to move more quickly and dramatically than the price of the ordinary share itself, thus magnifying gains and increasing losses. When the option expires at the end of the stated period it is worthless. Your maximum loss is therefore the actual cost of the option, i.e. your total investment but the potential gains are usually larger than on the ordinary share itself. Any gains are subject to income tax at your highest rate.

- Commodities

These are physical goods such as foodstuffs, gold, silver and oil. There are markets around the world where these commodities are traded and the usual form of contract is a futures one. They are a high risk investment as often it is events which could not be foreseen which will determine their price, i.e. bad weather, a plague of insects etc.

- Property

Normally divided into residential and corporate, with the

latter being more risky. This is usually a long-term investment, involving a high outlay and any gains, after adjusting for inflation, are subject to capital gains tax unless the property is your main residence.

The first message to draw from Table Two is that you cannot hope to make your money grow without taking some degree of risk. If you are not prepared to take any risk with your savings then you have to opt for an investment which pays you interest in return for your cash. This may be fixed over a certain period or fluctuate. The second message is that you can boost the value of your savings by taking various degrees of risk and there is no need to opt for highly speculative investments. Finally, different levels of risk may be appropriate for your savings. Most of us will want to keep a certain sum on deposit for example and then divide the rest up according to temperament as well as other considerations.

Next, let's take a look at your time horizons. This is two fold – the length of time you are willing to save and your desire for accessability. Often the two are inextricably mixed as say for example with a ten year insurance policy where most of the benefits start clocking up after year five. In other cases such as unit trust or shares you may be able to get your money within weeks but the need to do so may seriously mar your investment performance or indeed not give your money sufficient time to grow in order to compensate for the charges involved in the purchase.

Of course there are no cast iron rules about time scale but the table is designed to give you a general flavour, indicating the average time it will take to recoup your buying charges and give your money some time to grow. For example, many people have made a profit within weeks buying new share issues. It also highlights the potential down side if you need instant access to your cash.

Choosing your route

Once you have decided which investments are best suited to your needs you need to examine the optimum way to invest

Table Three: Time Horizons

Investment	Access	Suitable timescale	Withdrawal penalties
Deposit account	Immediate	7 days to 3 years	Loss of interest equal to notice period
National Savings	Subject to product	One month to 5 years	Varies depending on product from loss of interest over notice period to lower interest rate on savings
Government securities	Within one week	In excess of 6 months	Possible loss of proportion of capital
Corporate bonds	Within 3 weeks	In excess of 6 months	Possible loss of capital
Ordinary shares	Within 3 weeks	In excess of one year	Possible loss of capital
Futures	Within 3 weeks	Days up to years	Possible loss greater than initial outlay
Options	Within 3 weeks	Days up to months	Possible loss of capital
Property	Months subject to negotiation	Several years	Possible loss of capital
Commodities	Negotiable	Days up to years	Possible loss of capital

Notes: Government securities, corporate bonds and ordinary shares are subject to the settlement rules of the Stock Exchange. Government securities are dealt on a cash basis, i.e. transactions are paid for at the time completed whereas shares are bought and sold on credit over the Scotk Exchange account. Most accounts run for two weeks, although there are two three week accounts. Your broker will be able to give you a timetable.

Futures and options are traded on a number of markets both here and abroad. The dealing costs and settlement term vary according to each individual market.

Property cannot be sold quickly and must therefore be regarded as a very long term investment. The paperwork alone may take up to two months.

in them to boost your after tax return. You should at this stage take into account whether you wish to manage your own investments and if not, how you wish to delegate the decision making. You may for example prefer a packaged investment where the advice is left to the managers or to seek advice on direct investments. Much will depend upon the sums involved as unfortunately finding advice for a small amount of money can be virtually impossible at worst and horribly expensive at best. In the investment world a small sum means less than tens of thousands of pounds.

Let us show how this works by looking at the various ways you might choose to invest in shares. Each route is taxed differently and the charges vary which will affect your ultimate return. Table Four shows you the varying returns depending upon the route you pick of investing £1,000 in ordinary shares which rise by 5% per annum in price over ten years and which pay out a gross income of 5% over the same timespan. The investor pays 27% basic rate tax and no capital gains tax as his profits fall within his exempt allowance.

If there were no charges and no taxes then your return would be 10.25% per annum, but as you can see from Table Four you can do much better than that by choosing a pension or much worse by opting for an insurance bond. The lump sum at the end of ten years you receive from your pension is more than double the lump sum if you had opted for the insurance bond. As you can see, the way you invest is equally important as what you choose to invest in. Other things being equal, pension plans win hands down, that's because you receive tax relief on your investment and the funds are allowed to grow tax free. In addition, the lump sum payument at the end of the day is tax free within statutory limits. Unfortunately you cannot just withdraw your pension when you wish but have to wait until the agreed retirement date in your pension plan. Personal Equity Plans come second. Here your money is allowed to grow tax free and there is no additional tax bill on receipt. The main proviso being that the money has been invested for a full calendar year, i.e. from January 1 through to December 31.

Table Four: Comparative Investment Returns

SUMMARY – after 10 years	Ordinary shares	PEP	Unit trust	Investment trust	Insurance bond	Pension plan
Total value, before capital gains tax	£2,251.69	£2,287.95	£2,000.59	£2,251.69	£1,818.11	£3,284.11
Capital gains tax	0.00	0.00	0.00	0.00	0.00	0.00
Total value, after capital gains tax	£2,251.69	£2,287.95	£2,000.59	£2,251.69	£1,597.22*	£3,284.11
% return	8.46%	8.63%	7.18%	4.79%	6.17%	12.63%
Total tax paid	£203.33	£0.00	£189.68	£203.33	£562.74	£0.00

Source: Save & Prosper, July 1987.

Notes: Assumes you invested £1,000 and the performance achieved was uniform before tax deductions. Basic rate tax relief was granted on pensions at 27%. The following charges were deducted:

Ordinary shares   3.3% initial (i.e, 2x1.65% for buying and then selling)
Personal equity plan   2.25% initial, 0.625% each half year
Unit trust   5% initial, 1% annual
Investment trust   3.3% initial
Insurance bond   5% initial, 0.75% annual
Pension plan   5% initial, 0.5% annual

*Income tax is payable equal to £220.89

107

So much for a basic rate taxpayer, but what happens when you are a higher rate taxpayer and your gains are subject to capital gains tax at 30%? We redid the figures in Tables Five and Six to give you some idea of how these higher rates of tax will affect your return. Table Five looks at the position for someone in the 40% bracket and Table Six for someone in the 60% bracket, both pay capital gains tax.

These tables emphasise the point that the more tax you pay the more vital it is that you go for tax efficient investments and try to reduce the element of your return which is subject to the highest marginal rate of tax, i.e. the income. To show you the importance of this latter point we have reworked the figures in Table Four, i.e. for basic rate taxpayer whose profits are tax free as they fall within the capital gains tax exempt band and assumed that the return on the investment was purely in the form of growth with no income. We have assumed a 10% rate of capital growth on the underlying investments in Table Seven.

The results from Table Seven show a change in the pecking order. Here the lower charges involved in direct equity investments, i.e. buying shares or investment trusts, outweigh the tax advantages of the personal equity plan. What's more the differential between the unit trust and the personal equity plan has virtually disappeared.

The investment world is highly competitive and charges for certain products such as unit trusts and insurance bonds are pretty standard. However, in other areas such as pensions and personal equity plans where there are strong tax incentives, charges may vary more dramatically and this will obviously affect your return.

Obviously when you come to decide which company's product to choose you need to look at their actual investment performance in the past, the company's philosophy and stability. However, in deciding how to structure your portfolio, general tax considerations should be taken into account.

Table Five: Comparative Investment Returns

SUMMARY – after 10 years	Ordinary shares	PEP	Unit trust	Investment trust	Insurance bond	Pension plan
Total value, before any tax on gains	£2,113.85	£2,287.95	£2,000.59	£2,113.85	£1,818.11	£3,995.67
Personal CGT	−334.16	0.00	−300.18	−334.16	0.00	0.00
(or) income tax	0.00	0.00	0.00	0.00	−327.24	0.00
Total value, after any tax on gain	£1,779.70	£2,287.95	£1,700.41	£1,779.70	£1,490.87	£3,995.67
% return on investment	5.93%	8.63%	5.45%	5.93%	4.07%	14.86%
Total tax paid	£625.25	£0.00	£489.86	£625.25	£669.09	£0.00

Source: Save & Prosper, July 1987

Table Six: Comparative Investment Returns

SUMMARY – after 10 years	Ordinary shares	PEP	Unit trust	Investment trust	Insurance bond	Pension plan
Total value, before any tax on gains	£1,917.33	£2,287.95	£2,000.59	£1,917.33	£1,818.11	£5,993.50
Personal CGT	−275.20	0.00	−300.18	−275.20	0.00	0.00
(or) income tax	0.00	0.00	0.00	0.00	−490.87	0.00
Total value, after any tax on gain	£1,642.13	£2,287.95	£1,700.41	£1,642.13	£1,327.24	£5,993.50
% return on investment	5.09%	8.63%	5.45%	5.09%	2.87%	19.61%
Total tax paid	£689.62	£0.00	£489.86	£689.62	£832.72	£0.00

Source: Save & Prosper, July 1987

Table Seven: Comparative Investment Returns

SUMMARY – after 10 years	Ordinary shares	PEP	Unit trust	Investment trust	Insurance bond	Pension plan
Total value, before any tax on gains	£2,508.15	£2,236.59	£2,228.45	£2,508.15	£1,808.46	£3,210.39
Personal CGT	0.00	0.00	0.00	0.00	0.00	0.00
(or) income tax	0.00	0.00	0.00	0.00	–218.28	0.00
Total value, after any tax on gain	£2,508.15	£2,236.59	£2,228.45	£2,508.15	£1,590.17	£3,210.39
% return on investment	9.63%	8.38%	8.34%	9.63%	4.75%	12.37%
Total tax paid	£0.00	£0.00	£0.00	£0.00	£539.12	£0.00

Source: Save & Prosper, July 1987

Packaged deals

Not all investments can be packaged in the same way as shares. For example, let's say you wanted to invest in government securities, your options would be to invest direct, via a unit trust, through an offshore fund, within your pension fund or insurance bond. You cannot use your personal equity plan to buy government stocks and there is no investment trust currently listed in London which invests in such stocks. Table Eight indicates the type of investments which can be packaged in various ways.

Table Eight: Inside the package

Product	Potential underlying investments
Investment trust	Stocks, shares, unquoted companies, property, commodity, futures, options, cash, currencies.
Personal Equity Plan	75% UK listed shares, up to 25% authorised unit trusts or listed investment trusts.
Pension	Stocks, shares.
Offshore fund	As specified in company's prospectus.
Unit trust	Stocks, shares, gilts and bonds.

The government is currently considering proposals to lift the restrictions on authorised unit trusts and permit them to invest in a wider range of products but no date has been announced.

There is one more factor which needs to be highlighted in packaged investments and that's the hidden risk factor which may be involved if the manager has the capacity to borrow. This is known as gearing because your money is geared up by additional funds. If the cost of the borrowing is less than the return the manager earns on the money then the investors overall return is boosted, if not then it is decreased. Table

111

Nine shows you which products are permitted to gear up their funds.

Table Nine: Gearing Up

Product	Gear
Personal equity plans	No
Investment trusts	Yes
Unit trusts	No
Insurance bonds	Not generally
Pension plans	Not generally
Offshore funds	Possibly, but not generally

Flexibility

One factor to keep in mind when planning your finances is that today's top investment opportunity may be tomorrow's winner of the wooden spoon. When you choose a packaged investment the charges are naturally higher than buying direct as you are paying for the fund manager's expertise and the administrative cost of running your plan. These costs are lumpy and the majority are usually deducted initially which means that switching between products can be costly. It is therefore useful to consider at the outset the flexibility of any plan, the cost of switching between different areas of investment and the tax implications.

The cost will vary from company to company and may depend on the number of switches over a specified period. Even if the switches are said to be 'free' there is usually a hidden fee to cover transaction costs, which can vary from 2% up to 13%. In addition you need to consider the capital gains tax position. You can swop inside a pension, personal equity plan or insurance bond without generating a capital gain for tax purposes but not between unit trust, shares and investment trusts. One loophole is offshore 'funds of funds' where you can swop tax free between sub-funds.

Further Reading

Beat The Money Trap by Rosemary Burr, Margaret Dibben and Wendy Elkington. Price £3.95. MOre than three hundred ways to make your money go further.

Unit Trusts Explained: The Easy Way To Buy Shares by Rosemary Burr. Price £3.99.

Guide to Personal Equity Plans by Rosemary Burr. Price £3.99.

Abbey Financial Rights Handbook by Wendy Elkington. Price £5.95.

More Shares For Your Money: A Guide To Buying Investment Trust Companies Shares by Christing Stopp. Price £5.95.

CHAPTER EIGHT:
FUTURE PERFECT

Retirement has been called the longest holiday of a lifetime, but few of us think about it with quite the same relish and enthusiasm as our fortnight in the sun. In fact, many people ignore the whole issue altogether in a rather vain hope that it will solve itself. Ideally we should consider retirement planning as a way of increasing our options, so that we can afford to retire at a time to suit ourselves and our families and then lead the sort of life we wish. In order to go at least some way towards meeting our objectives we need to plan sooner, rather than later.

Measuring your needs

The first step is to look at your current pension provision. Most of us are locked into the state system and perhaps the pension scheme where we work. The self employed and those who work for companies who do not run a pension scheme may have bought their own personal pensions.

Table One gives you an indication of what you can expect to receive from the state assuming you have a full National Insurance contribution record. Your state pension will consist of the basic pension and the earnings related portion known as SERPS, State Earnings Related Pension Scheme. As part of a complete overhaul of the state system benefits under SERPS will be reduced for those retiring after the year 2000 and an incentive bonus scheme will operate over the next five years to encourage people to opt out of SERPS by buying their own personal pensions.

The figures in Table One assume you are employed and

reliant on the state or self employed without a personal pension. The company where you work may run a scheme which you have been forced to join. This scheme may replace the SERPS element of the state provision in which case you pay lower National Insurance contributions to the government and channel money into your company scheme. Such a scheme is called 'contracted out' and has to provide you with at least as good benefits as the existing SERPS scheme. Other companies run schemes which are funded in parallel to your state pension. They do not replace SERPS but are an extra. These are called contracted in schemes and the benefits you ultimately receive are usually related to the investment performance of your contributions and your employees.

So much for what the state and your company will provide, but will this be sufficient to maintain your current lifestyle, even at today's prices? The answer is 'unlikely'. Table Two will help you show where you stand in the pension stakes at the moment. To fill it in you need to make certain assumptions about the type of lifestyle you plan to enjoy on retirement. If for example you expect to stay in the same property and live pretty much in the way to which you have grown accustomed it is best to assume you would need around 70% of your current income. Many people will have made no pension provision, so they can skip the line for their existing arrangements. If you belong to an occupational scheme or have made private arrangements already, i.e. bought a self employed plan, you may need to contact the people running the scheme to help you fill in this figure.

Table One: State Pension Benefits

Self-employed

Single	Married couple
£2,054	£3,289

Employed

Annual earnings	Expected total annual State Pension Benefits	
	Single	Married Couple
£ 6,000	£3,047	£4,282
£ 8,000	£3,547	£4,782
£10,000	£4,047	£5,282
£12,000	£4,547	£5,782
£14,000	£5,047	£6,282
£16,000 or over	£5,382	£6,617

Source: Save & Prosper, June 1987.

The above figures assume that:
1. Both self-employed and employed persons have full National Insurance Contribution record.
2. The employed persons will have at least 20 years in the SERPS since April 1978.

Table Two: Retirement Income Planner

Current age ....

Planned retirement age ....

Current earnings £ ....

If you retired today what percentage
of current income would you need .... %

Required retirement earnings £ ....

Current level of state pension £ ....

Existing pension provision £ ....

Total anticipated pension £ ....

SHORTFALL £ ....

118

Most of us will be staring at a rather nasty shortfall and that takes no account of any future rises in the cost of living. Now pensions are a very tax efficient form of investment. You receive tax relief on your contributions up to the statutory limit and the funds are allowed to grow tax free. On retirement you can divide your pension between a tax free lump sum, subject to a statutory ceiling, and a monthly income which will be taxable as earned income in your hands. There are broadly speaking two types of pension funds, those which relate the payout to your final salary and those which relate your payout to the actual return earned on your contributions. Occupational schemes may be of either sort, while personal pensions are usually of the latter type.

Up till April 1988 if you are in a job with an occupational scheme you had no choice but to contribute whatever proportion of your salary was included in your terms of employment and if the scheme included a so-called additional voluntary contribution option you could channel extra funds into your pension to take full advantage of the tax concessions. However, from April 1988 everyone will be free to opt out of their occupational scheme and each occupational scheme must by law permit its members to make additional contributions. There are also new rules which make it easier to transfer your money between schemes without being heavily penalised.

Those without an occupational pension or those who have decided to arrange their own will need to pick one of the new breed of personal pensions. A good pension plan apart from providing you with the staple pension should have the following features:

- Consistent long term performance
- Value for money
- Flexibility
- Easy to understand product
- Efficient after-sale service

The earlier you start the harder your money works for you. As a rough rule of thumb Table Three indicates how much

119

you should channel into your pension in order to produce an adequate income on retirement based on the number of years you make contributions.

Table Three: Building Up Your Pension

Period of contributions	Proportion of salary
40 years	5%
30 years	10%
20-25 years	15%
Under 20 years	As much as possible

With this greater degree of choice comes a whole range of new financial decisions which have to be taken but hopefully this greater freedom to take control of your pension arrangements should result in a better return. Since no two people's pension arrangements and future requirements are the same you should seek individual advice tailored to your own needs from a financial adviser specialising in pensions.

Planning tool

So much for the minimum requirement but since personal pensions are the most tax efficient form of investment open to us at the present it makes sense to make maximum use of them as a financial planning tool. It is here that personal pensions often score above occupational schemes because they give you greater scope to unlock the money which is being built up on your behalf inside the fund but which in normal circumstances cannot be touched until you retire. This facility is particularly important to businessmen as well as to those seeking a mortgage.

• Reducing company tax bill

Table Four shows how an executive pension scheme with a loan back facility can boost the company's resources while reducing the tax bill. Example A shows a company with gross profits of £120,000. This firm makes no pension arrangements for its key executives and so pays £34,400 by way of corporation tax. In example B the directors have decided to contribute £20,000 into a pension scheme which reduces their gross profit accordingly. They then pay less corporation tax and the £20,000 lump sum in the pension scheme has resulted in a reduction of only £2,600 in the company's retained profits. Finally in example C the directors have decided to unlock their pension contributions by arranging a loan thus boosting the amount retained within the company.

Table Four: Tax Cutting

	A No Pension Scheme	B Pension Scheme	C Pension Scheme with Loanback
Gross Profits	£120,000	£120,000	£120,000
Less Pension Contribution	Nil	£ 20,000	£ 20,000
Less Corporation Tax	£ 34,400*	£ 27,000	£ 7,000
Net profits retained in the Company	£ 85,600	£ 83,000	£ 83,000
Loanback to Company			£ 10,000
Amount retained in the Company after loanback			£ 93,000

```
*£100,000 @ 27% £27,000
 £ 20,000 @ 37% £ 7,400
                £34,400
```

Pension mortgages

As we have already seen in chapter five pension mortgages can be a very efficient method of paying for your home. Basically on reaching your retirement you take part of your pension as a tax free lump sum, which is used to repay the mortgage, and the rest as an annual income for life.

Since you obtain full tax relief on your pension contributions and the money is then permitted to grow tax free, the pension mortgage, especially for higher rate taxpayers, is an option well worth considering. The following four examples give you some indication of how the tax relief both on interest payments on mortgages up to £30,000 and on pension contributions within statutory limits make a pension mortgage so tax efficient for those paying higher levels of income tax.

Example One

A thirty-four year old man who plans to retire at sixty and wishes to take out a £30,000 mortgage. He pays tax at 40%. The calculations are based on the assumption that the low cost endowment policy grows by 10.25% and the underlying growth rate on the pension policy is 12% net of charges. The interest rate is 10.5%.

	Repayment mortgage	Low-cost endowment	Pension mortgage
Payment to lender	£204.82	£157.50	£157.50
Insurance policy premium	£6.20	£47.60	£4.86
Pension contribution	—	—	£50.50
Net monthly outlay	£211.02	£205.10	£212.86
Estimated cash surplus after mortgage repaid	Nil	£18,416	£7,500
Annual pension for life	Nil	Nil	£11,441

Source: Save & Prosper, July 1987.

In this instance the low cost endowment is the cheapest method of financing the mortgage, while a pension mortgage costs just under £2 more per month than a repayment mortgage.

Example Two

As example one, except the thirty-four year old now pays tax at 60%.

122

	Repayment mortgage	Low-cost endowment	Pension mortgage
Payment to lender	£169.88	£105.00	£105.00
Insurance policy premium	£6.20	£47.60	£3.24
Pension contribution	—	—	£33.68
Net monthly outlay	£176.08	£152.60	£141.92
Estimated cash surplus after mortgage repaid	Nil	£18,416	£7,500
Annual pension for life	Nil	Nil	£11,441

Source: Save & Prosper, July 1987.

Here the pension mortgage works out as the cheapest option, before taking into account the additional benefits you would receive by adopting this method. The repayment route costs 24% more than the pension mortgage per month net of tax.

Example Three

As above except the person seeking the mortgage is forty-nine years old, pays tax at 40% and plans to retire at sixty-five. The term of the mortgage here is fifteen years compared to the first two examples where the term was twenty-five.

	Repayment mortgage	Low-cost endowment	Pension mortgage
Payment to lender	£264.85	£157.50	£157.50
Insurance policy premium	£16.90	£122.20	£14.40
Pension contribution	—	—	£158.10
Net monthly outlay	£281.75	£279.70	£330.00
Estimated cash surplus after mortgage repaid	Nil	£9,446	£7,500
Annual pension for life	Nil	Nil	£11,441

Source: Save & Prosper, July 1987.

Here the cheapest option is the low cost endowment policy with the pension mortgage scoring badly since despite the tax concessions the person seeking the home loan has only fifteen years' worth of contributions until he is due to retire.

Example Four

As three except the person seeking the mortgage pays income tax at 60%. As you see for higher rate taxpayers the pension mortgage once again emerges as the cheapest option, giving a handy saving of £28 per month over the most expensive method of financing the home loan, the repayment morgage.

	Repayment mortgage	Low-cost endowment	Pension mortgage
Payment to lender	£232.12	£105.00	£105.00
Insurance policy premium	£16.90	£122.20	£9.60
Pension contribution	—	—	£105.40
Net monthly outlay	£248.02	£227.20	£220.00
Estimated cash surplus after mortgage repaid	Nil	£9.446	£7,500
Annual pension for life	Nil	Nil	£11,441

Source: Save & Prosper, July 1987.

Investment options

Pensions funds have a great deal of investment freedom and if you are choosing a personal plan, you should try to make maximum use of this flexibility. What is an appropriate investment for someone who has thirty years to go before retiring is not necessarily equally suitable for someone due to retire within the next few years. As with all investments you cannot afford to simply forget about your money. Generally speaking the further you are away from retirement the higher the risks you can afford to take, the nearer the lower.

Sources of further information

The Company Pensions Information Centre (CIPC),
7 Old Park Lane, London W1Y 3LJ.

The CPIC produces booklets available on request and accompanied by SAE (at least 7″ x 9″), and will try to answer questions of general principle on company pension schemes.

The National Association of Pension Funds (NAPF),
12-18 Grosvenor Gardens, London SW1W 0DH.

The NAPF publishes books and leaflets (some of them free) on a whole range of pensions matters. A publication list is available from the NAPF.

The Occupational Pensions Advisory Service (OPAS),
Room 327, Aviation House, 129 Kingsway, London
WC2B 6NN.

OPAS offers advice and assistance on pension scheme matters to individual elderly members of the public and others who are considered deserving by reason of their financial circumstances.

The Department of Health and Social Security (DHSS),
PO Box 21, Stanmore, Middlesex HA4 1AY.

The DHSS produces leaflets on all aspects of state pensions and social security benefits. For general information on social security matters, dial 100 and ask for Freephone DHSS.

CHAPTER NINE:
SCHOOL FEES

Roughly seven in every one hundred British children now go to a private school. School fees are not cheap, the average wage in 1986 was £9,500 per annum and the average cost of one year's boarding at a boy's senior private school was £4,725. Girl's schools are on average slightly cheaper and, of course, day schools are naturally less expensive too. Over the past four years private school fees have risen faster than inflation as Table One shows.

Table One: School Fees

	Rise in school fees	Rise in RPI
1986	11%	3.9%
1985	9%	6.1%
1984	7%	6.1%
1983	8%	5.0%

Source: ISIS

Notes: Based on figures up to January 1987.

In order to help you work out the future cost we have produced a table which assumes school fee prices will rise by varying degrees over the next ten years. These will give you a rough guide for your future needs and can be used when completing table three which assesses your total potential outlay.

Table Two: How Price Rises Bite

| Years | Projected termly costs after price rise per annum of | | |
	5%	10%	20%
1988	1,782.9	1,867.8	2,037.6
1989	1,872.0	2,054.5	2,445.0
1990	1,965.6	2,259.9	2,934.0
1991	2,063.8	2,485.8	3,520.8
1992	2,166.9	2,734.3	4,224.8
1993	2,275.2	3,007.7	5,069.6
1994	2,388.9	3,308.4	6,083.4
1995	2,508.3	3,639.2	7,300.0
1996	2,633.7	4,003.1	8,760.0
1997	2,765.3	4,403.4	10,512.0

Notes: Based on the average cost of private school fees for male boarders as at January 1987 of £1,698.

Apart from the basic fee, you will need to take account of a number of extras. These include uniforms, special lessons and additional expenses such as sports equipment and books. As a rough rule of thumb add between £300 and £1,000 per annum to your figures, although this will obviously vary if for example you have a musically gifted child. Table Three will help you estimate your requirements each year.

Income routes

Most people will be financing their children's school fees out of their income so it is a question of the most tax efficient way of producing the stream of income required, while providing your desired element of flexibility so that you can have access to the funds if you change your mind about sending your child to a particular private school. As with most investments the earlier you get cracking the less the pain. This is particularly true with school fees because

Table Three: Fees Planner

Year	Name of child(ren)	Total
Fees in		
Fees in		
Fees in		
Fees in		
Fees in		
Fees in		
Fees in		
Fees in		
Fees in		
Fees in		
	Total	

Source: Save & Prosper Group 1987.

contrary to the popular belief that your biggest investment is your home, your most costly single item of expenditure is school fees if you decide to go for private tuition. The average cost of a house today is £38,121, while sending your son to a top boarding school for eight years will cost £46,800 – and that's assuming that prices do not rise in the meantime.

In theory you could use any form of regular saving scheme to build up a lump sum. However in practice most advisers recommend that to make the most of your long term saving you use some form of equity investment preferably one which allows you to withdraw the cash tax-free as by the time your children are old enough to go to public school the chances are you will be paying higher rate tax. This reduces the choice dramatically to a series of endowment policies or personal equity plans.

There are several different types of endowment policy on the market but they do share two things in common. They include automatic life cover for the policyholder and to enjoy the maximum tax and investment benefits they should be regarded as ten year plans. The main choice you have to make is whether to opt for a so-called unit linked policy where your ultimate payout is linked to the direct value of your premiums which have been invested in the funds of your choice or whether to go for the more old fashioned with profits policy where you start with a guaranteed minimum and share the profits which have been built up in the general pool of managed funds by the insurance company.

Unit linked policies are rather like children in one way – when they are good, they are very, very good and when they are bad, they are awful. That's because your payout will depend upon the underlying fund's value at a specific date in time, namely when you wish to withdraw the cash, rather than reflect the gradual build up of profits. However you can soften this risk by switching between funds within your endowment policy and opting for deposit or gilt trusts as you get nearer the date you need the cash. Both types of endowment policy are taxed in the same way. Inside the fund profits and income are subject to corporation tax, currently 35%, but much of the income has effectively been taxed at the basic rate of income tax, i.e. 27%. Provided you leave your money inside the policy for seven and a half years your withdrawals are tax-free.

A potentially more tax efficient route is to link your school fee planning to a series of personal equity plans. Here your money inside the fund can grow completely free of tax and the withdrawal restrictions are less onerous. Provided you keep the funds locked inside the plan for a full calendar year, i.e. from January 1 to December 31 all the gains are tax free in your hand. However, there is a ceiling of £2,400 per annum which each individual can place in such funds. Both husband and wife are entitled to put in this sum.

Personal equity plans are essentially a higher risk form of investment than endowment policies as 90% of the money must remain invested in shares throughout the plan's life. What is more the bulk of the funds, 75% must be earmarked for the London stockmarket with up to 25% going into unit trusts or investment trusts through which you can obtain exposure to other international stockmarkets.

Pep versus endowment

To judge the impact on your cash flow of opting for a personal equity plan rather than a series of endowment policies, we have looked at two examples. In the first case the investor has a full ten years worth of saving and in the second instance only six years. We have compared the return from a maximum investment plan, which consists of a series of ten year unit linked life assurance policies plus a small element of life cover with that from a personal equity plan.

Example One: 10 years' savings for 5 years' schools fees

Year	Monthly Investment £	Maximum Investment Plan		Personal Equity Plan	
		Start year cash-in value £	School fees £	Start year cash-in value £	School fees £
1	100	—	—	—	—
2	100	471	—	1,226	—
3	100	1,726	—	2,601	—
4	100	3,097	—	4,141	—
5	100	4,597	—	5,868	—
6	100	6,378	—	7,804	—
7	100	8,206	—	9,974	—
8	100	10,268	3,205	12,406	3,807
9	100	9,011	3,205	10,865	3,807
10	100	7,630	3,205	9,138	3,807
11	—	6,112	3,205	7,203	3,807
12	—	3,205	3,205	3,807	3,807
13	—	—	—	—	—
Total School fees			16,025		19,035

Source: Save & Prosper Group, March 1987.

Example Two: 6 years' savings for 5 years' schools fees

Year	Monthly Investment £	Maximum Investment Plan		Personal Equity Plan	
		Start year cash-in value £	School fees £	Start year cash-in value £	School fees £
1	100	—	—	—	—
2	100	471	—	1,226	—
3	100	1,726	—	2,601	—
4	100	3,097	—	4,141	—
5	100	4,597	1,607	5,868	1,969
6	100	4,519	1,607	5,597	1,969
7	—	4,336	1,607	—	1,969
8	—	3,407	1,607	—	1,969
9	—	1,607	1,607	1,969	1,969
10	—	—	—	—	—
	Total School fees		8,035		9,845

Source: Save & Prosper Group, March 1987.

Notes:

Return: It has been assumed in line with the Association of British Insurers guidelines that the return on the Maximum Investment Plan is 10.75 per annum net of tax. This has been split between 3.5% net income and 7.25% capital growth net of tax at an effective rate of 15% to take indexation into account. On the Personal Equity Plan a total gross return of 13.5% has been assumed. This has been split between 4.0% gross income and 8.53% gross capital growth.

Charges: The charges on the Maximum Investment Plan are those included in the Save & Prosper contract and assume 99% allocation of your cash into units. On the Personal Equity Plan the return assumes an initial charge of 4% and a annual charge of 1¼% plus VAT.

Tax in Example Two: No account has been taken in the figures of any possible higher rate tax liability on partial withdrawals from a Maximum Investment Plan before year seven and a half. Nor has any account been taken of any tax liability on withdrawals from a Personal Equity Plan within the first calendar year. In both cases the tax liability would be small.

Clearly the personal equity plan wins hands down over the maximum investment plan. In example one the return from the personal equity plan is 19.8% higher than the maximum

132

investment plan and in example two the return is 22.5% higher.

Another alternative would be to use a regular unit trust savings scheme to channel your investments into shares. Here the return for basic rate taxpayers who do not expect to pay capital gains tax in the relevant period when they would be making encashments is marginally lower than on the personal equity plan.

If you are not happy with the risks involved in shares, then you may prefer to consider a series of government securities. Gains on gilts are tax free but the income is subject to income tax. Gilts are issued in units of £100 and carry a guarantee of repayment by a certain date. For instance, Treasury 3000 would be repaid in the year 3000. The government usually tries to cater for all tastes and will issue some gilts substantially below par, i.e. at less than £100 which may carry a lower coupon or interest rate.

It is something of a historical quirk that if you give money to someone under a deed of covenant then certain tax advantages may flow. A deed of covenant is a legal agreement and in order to be valid must be completed and sealed in a specified manner. Under the current rules there are tax advantages to the recipient in the following cases:

- if the money is given by anyone other than their parents or spouses
- if they are over eighteen or married and the money is given by a parent

In terms of financing your child's education the main benefits occur if you can persuade a grandparent, friend or relative to covenant your child money up to the age of eighteen and beyond, and if you covenant money to your student offspring over the age of eighteen. Provided these conditions are met and the sum covenanted does not bring your child's income above the single person's allowance in the relevant tax year then every £730 given is turned into £1,000 in the child's hands.

The Inland Revenue produces a useful free information

133

pack, IR59 called Students Tax Information Pack, which explains how covenants work, how to claim your tax relief and gives sample forms. It also publishes a free leaflet, Deeds of Covenant, 'Getting it right for tax' (IR74) which spells out the legal requirements clearly. This leaflet was brought out in July 1987 to help people draw up valid covenants and stop tax fiddles. Many investment companies also provide forms which can be used to channel covenanted money into a range of their products. Using this approach can substantially boost the return on your investments for relatively little hassle. However, remember to make sure the deed of covenant is properly executed – you may need to consult your solicitor – and that in theory the person covenanting the cash is making a seven year commitment.

Capital routes

If you are lucky enough to have a lump sum which you can invest to pay for future school fees then it makes sense to take advantage of tax concessions granted to charitable trusts. Many individual public schools have set up arrangements for this purpose, known as school fees composition schemes. Here your money is invested and allowed to grow tax free inside the fund. When you need to start withdrawing income the accumulated cash is used to purchase an annuity which pays a stated sum of income each year. The income is tax free but you do effectively forfeit your capital. That said this system can reduce the eventual costs of your school fees by up to 66%. Unless you are adamant about the eventual school your child will go to it is wisest to opt for an educational trust run by an independent specialist such as insurance company. Table Eight shows how this system can reduce your costs.

Table Eight assumes that you invest £10,000 in the Save & Prosper School Fees Capital Plan and that you will need to start making withdrawals to fund your child's education in eight years time. Based on rates as at March 1987 your £10,000 would be guaranteed to provide a stream of income of £4,845 for a period of five years. The actual sum you would

Table Seven: Do's and Don'ts for Deeds of Covenant

DO	DON'T
1. seek professional advice or use the forms provided by the Inland Revenue for student covenants or by charities for charitable donations.	1. backdate a deed – the date on it must be the date you actually made it.
2. make sure the covenant can last for more than six years, or more than three years if it is to a charity.	2. alter the deed in any way.
3. make the correct payments under the terms of the deed.	3. get involved in any arrangements with one or more other parents to provide equivalent benefits for your respective children.
4. give the recipient a form R185 (AP) New for every payment you make.	4. make a deed of covenant in exchange for cash, goods, services or other benefits supplied by anyone.
5. if you receive payments under a covenant claim tax relief only on sums actually received.	5. get involved in arrangements in which someone making a covenant is paid back, either directly or indirectly, for the payments made.
6. remember to send the forms R(185) New with your claim for tax relief.	6. do or give anything in return for the payments.
	7. include special powers to cancel the deed.

Table Eight: Capital Plan

Marginal tax rate	Fees providing for 5 years starting in 8 years time from a £10,000 investment		Amount of gross income freed-up	
%	Each Year £	Total £	Each Year £	Total £
27	4,845	24,225	6,636	33,180
40	4,845	24,225	8,075	40,315
45	4,845	24,225	8,810	44,050
50	4,845	24,225	9,690	48,450
55	4,845	24,225	10,765	53,825
60	4,845	24,225	12,110	60,550

Source: Save & Prosper Group, March 1987, based on the group's School Fees Capital Plan.

save by opting for this method rather than simply paying the same level of fees out of taxed income depends of course on how much income tax you would pay. The higher your rate of income tax the greater the saving, but even basic rate taxpayers would see a 27% saving over the five year period.

How does the scheme work? Well, your lump sum payment is used to buy an annuity which effectively turns your capital into a stream of income. This income in turn is paid out to the school of your choice at the date agreed. It does not count as part of your taxable income under current Inland Revenue practice. What's more it is a guaranteed sum which you can calculate at the outset. Most schemes are flexible enough to include the chance to provide increasing payments over the period which hopefully will be sufficient to offset rises in fees which may occur at a later date.

Other sources of help

● The school itself

Most schools provide places at reduced fees for very able children or those which fall into specified categories, e.g. the offspring of the clergy, armed forces etc. You should contact the bursar at the school of your choice for details or consult some of the publications listed at the end of this chapter.

- Government grants

If you work overseas for the diplomatic service your child will be able to obtain a grant to cover a portion of the costs. Details are available from the Foreign and Commonwealth Office.

If you are a member of Her Majesty's Forces, serving either at home or abroad, then you can obtain an allowance against the cost of boarding. Details can be obtained from the Service Children's Education Authority, Court Road, Eltham, London SE9 5NR.

Low income families, currently those earning less than £16,000, with bright children may qualify for a central government grant, see Table Nine. In 1986 25,000 such grants, totalling £34m, were given. Roughly two fifths of the grants were to families earning less than £6,972 and covered the whole cost of the child's school fees, while a further fifth were to families earning less than £8,000 per annum. Details are available from the Department of Eduation and Science, Room 3/65, Elizabeth House, York Road, London SE1 7PH. Tel: 01-934 9211 or the Welsh Office Education Department, Cathays Park, Cardiff CF1 3NQ. Tel: 0222 823347. Scotland has its own scheme. For further details please contact Scottish ISIS, 22 Hanover Street, Edinburgh EH2 2EP. Tel: 031-225 7202.

- Your employer

A few international companies have set up schemes to help their employees who work abroad finance their child's education at home. They vary from company to company and may simply take the form of a loan. If this is the case the tax considerations should be examined carefully. If you are a director or earn more than £8,500 per year then you will pay income tax at your highest rate on the interest element you would have paid if the loan had been arranged through normal commercial channels.

Table Nine: Assisted Places Scheme: Scales of Income

Parents' contribution to Fees: 1987-88 School Year		
Relevant income 1986/87 tax year (after allowances for dependants)	One assisted place holder	For each of two assisted place holders
£	£	£
6,972	Free	Free
7,000	15	12
8,000	123	93
9,000	273	204
10,000	471	354
11,000	681	510
12,000	921	690
13,000	1,161	870
14,000	1,449	1,086
15,000	1,779	1,335
16,000	*2,109	1,581

Notes: These scales were fixed in Spring 1987 and will be updated in Spring 1988. The income is gross income before tax deductions but families may deduct £900 (currently under review) for each child (or dependent relative) other than the candidate.

These scales are for the 1987/88 academic year and will probably be increased in line with inflation for the 1988/89 academic year.

*The maximum relevant income at which pupils will be eligible for assistance will vary in relation to schools' fees. In many schools the fees will not be as high as this and where this is so parents at this level of income will be ineligible.

● Professional associations

If you are a member of a professional association you may be able to get help. Contact the national secretary of the appropriate body.

● Local authorities

Funds from local authorities are very limited and only 8,000 pupils obtained financial assistance from this source in 1986, and policy varies from authority to authority. Apply direct to the director of education or chief education officer in your area. You may in certain circumstances also be able to obtain help from the LEA.

- Grant giving trusts

These are a last resort for people with genuine need who cannot find help elsewhere. Details are to be found in The Director of Grant Making Trusts, published by the Charities Aid Foundation and available in more public libraries.

CHAPTER TEN:
THE MONEY MULTIPLIER

Ask any investment adviser or financial journalist what is the most common request they receive and the answer is guidance on lump sum investment. The money may be part of an

Table One: Investment Planner

1. Investment objective
 	
    Capital growth
    High income
    Income and growth	

2. Time scale for investment
 	
  e.g. Short-term
       Long-term	

3. Accessibility
 	
  e.g. Immediate access
       Long-term commitment	

4. Attitude to risk
 	
  e.g. Low
       Moderate
       Speculative	

5. Tax position
 	
    On income
    On capital gains	

Source: Save & Prosper Group, 1987.

inheritance, a gift or a redundancy payment and obviously the solutions have to be tailored to meet the individual's existing circumstances, personal preferences and aims. Table One will help you define your objectives.

● Investment objectives

Most people will have a number of objectives and these may clash. So you will need to sort out your order of priorities. The checklist below will help.

---

1. Do you need to use some of the money to boost your current income? Yes/No

2. If yes, by how much would you like to increase your income? £ ....

3. Over what period of time will you need this income? ....

4. Will this income supplement or replace your regular earnings? ....

5. Do you wish to build up a lump sum for the future? Yes/No

6. Is there any specific date when you will need to use this money? Yes/No

7. If there is a specific date, what is it? ....

8. Can you affort to leave the money untouched without adversely hitting your future lifestyle? Yes/No

9. Are you prepared to put all the money at risk? Yes/No

10. If no, is there a certain proportion you are prepared to risk? .... %

The way you answer the above questions will determine

how you fill in the form. Let's say you have inherited £30,000 and out of this sum you wish to pay for your two children's school fees, improve your home and employ a nanny. You would fill in the questions as follows:

1. Yes
2. £4,000 per annum
3. The next four years
4. Supplement
5. Yes
6. Yes
7. In ten years time
8. Yes, that part not used to pay for the nanny
9. No
10. Yes, that part not used for the nanny

Now let us see if it is possible to realise your objectives. You deduct £3,000 at the outset to improve your home which leaves you with £27,000 to invest. Out of this sum you want to provide an income of £4,000 per annum over the next four years. You can check the current rate of interest on a bank or building society for a rough estimate. Let's say you can earn 10% net on your cash in a high interest account. If you then left the £27,000 on deposit you would generate £2,700 per annum which is not sufficient for your purposes. As an alternative you could use some of the capital itself.

Table Two: On Deposit

| | Capital | Withdrawals financed by | |
		Deposit interest	Capital
Year One	£27,000	£2,700	£1,300
Year Two	£25,700	£2,570	£1,430
Year Three	£24,270	£2,427	£1,573
Year Four	£22,697	£2,269	£1,731
Year Five	£20,966	—	—

The trouble with adopting this approach is that your savings are shrinking. Let us see what happens if you try a different tack. Reserve £16,000 to pay for the nanny over the next four years and place this sum in a high interest account. Then invest the remainder for growth. The interest earned reduces the need to eat into your capital.

● Bank or building society account

| | Capital | Withdrawals financed by | |
		Deposit interest	Capital
Year One	£16,000	£1,600	£2,400
Year Two	£13,400	£1,340	£2,660
Year Three	£10,740	£1,074	£2,926
Year Four	£7,814	£781	£3,219
Year Five	£4,595	—	—

● Invest £11,000 in growth orientated unit trusts assuming average annual return of 13% net of tax. By the end of year four this sum will have grown to £17,808. Add this amount to the cash you would have left in your deposit account and you have a total of £22,403. That's a larger sum than if you had simply placed your £27,000 at the outset on deposit.

So when filling in your investment objective instead of simply saying high income you should put two ticks, one next to capital growth and one next to high income and write the appropriate sum next to each category.

The same general principle applies to those who are retired and wish to live off a lump sum and those made redundant. First make sure you can satisfy your immediate income requirements and then go for maximum growth with the remainder of your money.

● Time scale

It is best to assume the worst possible case when filling out the timescale. Generally people tend to underestimate their needs for ready cash and ignore those emergencies which are bound to crop up – repairing the car, fixing something which goes wrong in your home etc. You should always try and leave yourself with a money cushion by placing on deposit in an instant access account a sum equal to two months earnings.

● Accessability

The longer you can tie up your money, the better the return. By giving up instant access you can often opt for more tax efficient investments. Again do not be over optimistic. If at the outset you choose a long term plan such as say a ten year insurance policy and find in several years time you have to cash it in you may receive less than you invested.

● Attitude to risk

You cannot hope to see your money grow without taking at least some level of risk. If you want to protect your capital completely then you will have to opt for bank, building society or National Savings accounts which pay interest and return your capital intact. However, remember that even if inflation is only running at 5% per annum, low by historical standards, £1,000 in five years time will have decreased its purchasing power by about 22%.

● Tax position

Even if you need extra income your tax position may vitally alter the way you should plan your investments. Currently each person has an annual capital gains tax allowance of £6,600 and after that gains, adjusted for inflation, are taxed at 30%. Income tax rates range from 27% up to 60%.

Higher rate taxpayers can therefore boost their overall return by opting for growth investments rather than income ones. Let's say you pay tax at 40% and assume you can earn a 10% gross income or a 10% growth rate on your money. If you choose the income route you will end up with an after-tax income of just £600 and no increase in your capital. However, if you opt for the capital growth route you can still enjoy an income of £600 per annum by making annual tax-free capital withdrawals, pay no tax and see the value of your capital rise.

Table Three: Income Route

		Income gross	Return after 40% tax
Year One	£10,000	£1,000	£600
Year Two	£10,000	£1,000	£600
Year Three	£10,000	£1,000	£600
Year Four	£10,000	£1,000	£600
Total tax bill £2,400			
Value of deposit after four years £10,000			

Table Four: Capital Route

		Growth at 10%	Minus £600pa tax free
Year One	£10,000	£11,000	£10,400
Year Two	£10,400	£11,440	£10,840
Year Three	£10,840	£11,924	£11,324
Year Four	£11,324	£12,476	£11,876
Total tax bill Nil			
Value of holding after four years £11,876			

So you can see that the way you are taxed.will affect your investment objectives. Even if you need income as a high rate taxpayer it is often better to satisfy that need by going for investments which aim for growth.

146

The size of the sum to be invested is also crucial. Nearly all investments have a minimum and this can vary from a few pounds right up to several thousand pounds. The larger the amount the greater the choices and often the more complex the decision. On bigger sums the overall impact of any investment strategy on your tax position is likely to be significant and may result in a need for a complete overhaul of your existing investments.

Capital growth

In broad terms there are two basic ways to generate growth by putting your money either into companies or property. Of course if you know something about antiques or jewellery you may be able to make a killing on the art market but unless you are an aficionado such pastimes are best kept to the level of a hobby – which is not to say that you cannot make a profit but simply that you cannot rely on clocking up any gains. There is also the fascinating, diverse and complex field of commodities – but again this is best left to the professional player unless you have a particularly strong interest and feel for these markets. For most people an investment indirectly through the companies which make, produce or package these commodities is probably the best route.

Before taking the plunge you need to obtain an overall picture of your situation. Do you own your own home? Do you have money in bank accounts or building society accounts? Do you already own shares? What sector of the economy do you work in? One of the key principles of investment is to spread your risk. So it would not make sense for the long term security of your family if say you had a large mortgage, worked as a property developer and then placed your nest egg in a residential property fund. All your money would be tied up in bricks and mortar, difficult to cash in quickly and any downturn in the property market would hit not just your livelihood but your future style of life.

Fill in the list on the next page:

Table Five: Asset Checklist

Asset	Value	% of total
Home		
Deposit accounts		
Other property		
Stocks and shares		
Government securities		
Packaged share investments, i.e. unit trusts, endowment plans		
Total		100

Let's look at two people, Mr Land and Mr Stock. They are both professionals paying 45% rate income tax and have inherited £40,000. They are single, have made full use of their pension entitlements and are looking for long term growth from cash. Mr Land is a property developer and his home is worth £100,000. He has a few thousand pounds in a bank account, runs a small overdraft and £5,000 worth of

Table Six: Growth Strategies

	Mr Land	%	Mr Stock	%
Property	£100,000	95.2	£75,000	71.4
Shares	Nil	0	£25,000	23.8
Government securities	£5,000	4.8	Nil	0
National Savings	Nil	0	£5,000	4.8
Total	£105,000	100%	£105,000	100%

Note: Figures have been rounded to nearest decimal.

148

government securities. He owns no stocks and shares. Mr Stock has always enjoyed a flutter on the stockmarkets. His home is worth £75,000 and he has £15,000 worth of shares, £10,000 worth of unit trusts and £5,000 in tax free National Savings certificates. He rarely has any cash on deposit with the bank as he keeps a close eye on his cash flow.

Now the lump sum of £40,000 represents a huge boost to both Mr Stock and Mr Land's net worth, but the way they invest it may be completely different.

(a) Mr Land

He would do best to consider first tax free investments such as National Savings and a personal equity plan. Then he should look at the best way to build up a share portfolio. He may prefer to give the money to a stockbroker to administer, run his own portfolio or opt for a packaged investment, such as unit trusts or life assurance linked plan.

(b) Mr Stock

He may wish to buy a bigger house, invest in some government securities and try some overseas investment through a unit trust specialising in say the Far East, Europe or America.

There are no hard and fast rules when it comes to investment but there are general principles which it pays to follow, unless you have a very strong hunch which gives you the confidence to break them.

- Spread your risk
- In the long term the return from equity investment exceeds the return on cash or gilts
- Protect the real value of your capital from inflation
- Reduce your tax liability
- Keep an eye on liquidity

Table Seven shows you at a glance the key features of various growth orientated investments.

Table Seven: Key Investment Features

Product	Type of Risk	Liquidity
Ordinary shares	I/E/S	Very
Gilts	E/S	Very
Property	E/S	Poor
Commodities	I/E/S	Varies
Gold	E/S	Medium
Antiques	I/S	Medium/Poor

I: integral risk.   E: economic risk.   S: sentiment risk.

Three types of risk are identified separately although they are usually intertwined. The integral risk involved in the investment itself, i.e. if you buy shares in a company the risk of it going bust. The economic risk, i.e. that your return will be affected by general economic conditions which will alter interest rates or currencies and hence indirectly the value of your holdings. The sentiment risk, i.e. when the stock market is going down even the value placed on a high performing growing company may also fall.

Now you can reduce your level of risk by spreading your investments between holdings in the same sector. For example, let's assume one in every hundred companies were to see its price fall by more than 50% and you have £10,000 to invest. If you put £10,000 into one share then you are risking in this instance £5,000. However, if you put £1,000 into each of 100 companies then your risk is cut at a stroke to £500. Of course, in real life it is not as simple as that but you can reduce your risk quite effectively through several packaged share investments without running up huge dealing costs. Of course, the reverse side of the coin is that you are also likely to reduce your potential profit but it is up to everyone to make their own decision on how much risk they are prepared to take in order to achieve a higher return.

Liquidity is also vital as the more liquid an investment the quicker you can have access to your money and the more nimble you can be when responding to changing conditions. Investors in property appear to have short memories and many seem to forget the problems of the early 1970's when it was not simply a matter of static house prices, but bargain basement prices.

● Income

In many ways investing for income is rather easier that growth, if only because the risks and rewards are usually easier to quantify at the outset. You can either choose those products where your capital remains intact, those where it is at risk or those where you give up the right to your cash in return for a stream of income.

Table Eight: Risk and Volatility Factors

Product	Capital at risk	Capital returned on withdrawal
Bank or building society deposit account	No	Yes
National Savings Investment Account or Income Bonds	No	Yes
Income bonds issued by insurance companies	No	Yes
Government securities	Yes	Yes, subject to price of stock
Annuity	—	No
Shares, Investment trusts and	Yes	Yes, subject to price of the shares or units
Insurance bonds	Yes	Yes, subject to value of your holding. Withdrawals of up to 5% of value permitted tax free for up to twenty years.

The simplest option is to put your money on deposit with a bank, building society or National Savings. They will tell you how much interest they are prepared to pay and how much notice you must give before withdrawing the cash. The rate of interest may be fixed for a stated period or more likely the rate can be changed whenever the company wishes after giving you due notice. In some cases you will be paid a higher rate of interest if you agree to lock your money away for a lengthy period, say two years or more.

The next alternative is to go for an income bond issued by an insurance company, which is similar to a deposit except that you will be quoted a rate of interest at the outset which will be paid over a given number of years and you cannot withdraw your money until the end of the stated period.

Government securities, known as gilts can also be used to generate an income. These are issued in units of £100 and the income which will be paid on each unit, unless it is index-linked, is fixed from the outset. For example, Treasury 1989 5% would pay an income each year of £5 per unit and holders would receive £100 per unit in the year 1989.

The point to remember about gilts is that you always know two things – the amount of money you earn in interest each year and the price you will be paid for the gilt on maturity. What you don't know is what will happen to the price of the gilt in the intervening period.

An annuity is a policy issued by an insurance company which converts your capital into income. The amount of income you receive from any given capital sum will depend upon your age, sex and will vary from company to company. You can arrange for a fixed rate annuity, which pays the same amount for the rest of your life, or an increasing annuity, where the payout rises. You do not get your capital back.

You can obtain an income either from a direct investment in a company's shares or a packaged investment such as unit trusts or investment trusts. Here both the income and price you receive when you sell your shares or units are unknown. You have the chance to both enjoy a growing income and some capital growth, but the downside is that the amount of annual income may fall and you could lose some of your capital if shares prices decrease.

Insurance bonds is a life assurance contract with a very

Table Nine: Taxing Matters

Product	Income Paid	Tax due on Income	Tax reclaimable	Tax on capital
Bank/Building society deposits	Net of basic rate tax	Higher rate taxpayers have additional bill	No	No
National Savings Investment account and income bonds	Gross	Taxable at your rate of income tax	—	No
Income bonds	Net of basic rate tax	Higher rate taxpayers have additional bill	No	No
Government securities	Net of basic rate tax if purchased via broker. Gross if bought via post office.	Taxable at your rate of income tax	Yes	No
Annuity	Net of basic rate tax	Higher rate taxpayers have additional bill	Yes	—
Shares, investment trusts, unit trust	Net of basic rate tax	Higher rate taxpayers have additional bill	Yes	Yes, on gains in excess of annual capital gains tax allowance
Insurance bonds	Gross	On sale or maturity tax due is the difference between your rate of tax and the basic rate, i.e. a 60% taxpayer would pay 33%	No	Yes, at the same rate as tax on sums withdrawn as income

153

small protection element. It is basically an investment product. You can unlock some of the capital gains that are building up inside the bond by making withdrawals of up to 5% of the bond's value per year for up to twenty years.

The tax treatment of these various types of products is highlighted in Table Nine. If you do not pay income tax then try to steer clear of investments where you cannot reclaim the basic rate tax paid out on your behalf.

When picking investments for income remember that old bogey inflation and try to arrange a mix of products which give you some scope for a growing income over the years and at least the chance to maintain the real value of your capital. Although shares, unit trusts and investment trusts may provide you with a lower starting income than placing the equivalent sum in a building society they do give you the

Table Ten: The Growth Track

Year to 31 Dec.	Building Society		Income Trust	
	Income £	Capital £	Income £	Capital £
1964	333	10,000	0	9,500
1965	536	10,000	396	10,200
1971	650	10,000	487	15,680
1972	650	10,000	523	18,820
1973	808	10,000	606	13,620
1974	900	10,000	731	7,700
1975	871	10,000	828	16,300
1976	842	10,000	906	14,740
1982	1,003	10,000	1,860	30,040
1983	825	10,000	1,900	41,280
1984	849	10,000	2,018	54,300

Source: Unit Trust Association

Notes: Based on investment of £10,000 made in 1964. The initial charge on the income unit trust being 5%, reducing the capital value by £500 in year one.

chance to enjoy a rising income and capital growth. Table Ten gives you and example of how this has worked in the past over a timespan which included the stockmarket collapse of 1974.

If in 1964 you had put £10,000 in a building society account you would have earned a total income of £8,267 compared to an income of £10,255 on the same sum invested in an income unit trust. What's more the value of your capital would have more than quintupled if placed in the income trust and remained static if put on deposit with a building society.

A word of caution you may sometimes see advertisements offering very high guaranteed rates of interest for a specific number of years. Always check these very carefully, in the past a number of investors have lost their shirts by going for these seemingly cast iron guarantees. In fact, the companies making these promises then went bust and the guarantee was meaningless. If in any doubt consult your financial adviser.

CHAPTER ELEVEN:
GIVING IT AWAY

The government gets the chance to tax your money up to three times: when you earn it, when you invest it and when you give it to someone else. A vital part of financial planning is arranging how best to use your money not just to finance your own current expenditure and future needs but those of family and perhaps friends. In short, you need to check out the most tax efficient way of giving.

Tax-free gifts

Let us start with the easiest part of this tax jigsaw, those gifts which you can make without the taxman expecting a share. These are:

- gifts which are regarded as normal expenditure.
  These must be paid out of your taxed income, be made on a regular basis and not adversely hit your normal standard of living.

- gifts of up to £3,000 in a single tax year.
  This can be in the form of a single gift or several. You can carry forward any unused exemption each year to the following year when it will be used to boost that year's total provided that year's exemption has been used.

  So, for example, if in 1986/7 you only gave away £2,000 then in 1987/8 you could give away your annual limit of £3,000 plus £1,000 from the previous year. If you only gave away £1,000 in 1987/8 you could carry forward £2,000 from that year but not the £1,000 from 1986/7.

- small gifts of up to £250 per person.
  You can make as many of these as you wish but only one per recipient each year. The money is tax free provided the £250 ceiling is not breached. If you gave £260 then the whole sum would be taxable.

- wedding gifts.
  Each parent may give up to £5,000 as a marriage gift to their child, which includes stepchilden, adopted and illegitimate chilen. Grandparents are permitted to give up to £2,500 each and other people up to £1,000 each.

- gifts made during your lifetime for the maintenance of children and dependent relatives.
  This would include paying for your child's education or living expenses if he or she was either under 18 years of age or in full-time education. This also includes gifts made as part of a divorce settlement to support your children and ex-partner.

- gifts to recognised charities.

- gifts to political parties.
  If these are made on or within a year of death then the ceiling is £100,000 tax free.

- gifts for the public benefit or to support the nation's heritage.

- gifts of property including land, woodlands, works of art and historic homes.
  Certain conditions must be met by the recipient which will allow the general public to enjoy the property. A tax bill may fall due on the subsequent sale of such property at a later date.

Potentially exempt transfers, PETS

All other gifts made during your lifetime to individuals are not taxable straight away but may become liable to inheritance tax on your death. The operative word is here a 'gift' – it is very important that the money or assets are given without any strings attached and you do not subsequently receive any benefit from them. If you did receive some benefit then in techical parlance it would become a gift with reservation and be subject to inheritance tax, when you die.

Let us assume you make a gift of £3,000 to your godchild. It is an outright gift and therefore a PET. If you died within seven years the transfer would be liable to tax. Assuming you made no other gifts in the same tax year your £3,000 annual tax free allowance could be used retrospectively and no tax would be paid. If you survive a full seven years then the gift is no longer taxable. This is often called the 'seven year rule'.

Chargeable transfers

These are certain transfers of assets which are not made between individuals and are subject to tax at half the rate of inheritance tax straight away. The exact definition is a matter of case law and even the experts differ over this.

Inheritance tax

This tax was introduced in the Finance Act 1986 and covers all gifts or transfers of wealth, including your main residence, made on or after March 18, 1986. The key fact to remember is that it is designed to tax the sum transferred out of your estate not the value of the asset to the recipient. The tax can be paid either by you, the recipient or on your death out of the proceeds of your estate, the technical terms for your family wealth. Table One gives you an indication of the tax bill on specified sums.

As we have seen some gifts can be made tax free during your lifetime and others known coyly as PETs may be tax free if you survive a further seven years after the gift has been made and do not enjoy any financial benefit from the transaction. All other gifts are subject to tax and if you are a UK taxpayer this will include transfers of any property or

Table One: How Inheritance Tax Bites

Total assets liable	Tax liability
£	£
0-90,000	0
100,000	3,000
120,000	6,000
140,000	12,000
160,000	20,000
180,000	28,000
200,000	36,000
220,000	44,000
240,000	54,000
260,000	64,000
280,000	74,000
300,000	84,000
320,000	94,000
330,000	99,000

For estimates in excess of £330,000 take 60% of the excess and add £99,000 to find the tax liability.

financial assets which are held overseas since these too count as part of your estate.

Adding up your inheritance tax bill

The size of the tax bill on any gift is calculated on the loss of value to your estate. Let us say Uncle George gave you £9,000 but left you to settle up with the taxman. The Inland Revenue will receive less tax than if Uncle George settled the tax on the sum gifted. Uncle George pays inheritance tax at 30%. He gives you £9,000 and leaves you to settle with the taxman. Your tax bill is 30% of £9,000, i.e. £2,700 and your net legacy is £6,300.

However, if Uncle George decided to pay the taxman, he will be giving you £9,000 net of 30% tax. In fact, this is the equivalent of handing you over £12,857 gross. His tax bill will be 30% of £12,857, i.e. £3,857 and your net legacy will be £9,000.

Working out the bill is further complicated since some gifts are potentially taxable but only if you die within seven years and then on a sliding scale with the charge falling the longer you survive. Normally the person making a gift which is taxable straight away, i.e. does not fall into either the PET or tax exempt category will settle the tax bill, someone receiving a PET takes on the responsibility of paying any future tax bill and money distributed from a dead person's estate is given net of tax. In addition inheritance tax is charged on a band system with the first £90,000 being tax free. See Table Two.

Table Two: Inheritance Tax Rates

Taxable Transfer £000's	Slice £000's	Rate %	Tax on Slice £	Total Tax £
0-90	90	NIL	NIL	NIL
90-140	50	30	15,000	15,000
140-220	80	40	32,000	47,000
220-330	110	50	55,000	102,000
Over 330	—	60	—	—

As at June, 1987.

● Example

Let us see how these rules work out in practice. Mrs Jones is a widow with an estate valued at £210,000. She has two daughters and three grandchildren. She has decided to give some money to her grandchildren straight away. In her will she has left the residue of her estate to be shared equally between her two daughters.

Year One: Mrs Jones gives each of her three grandchildren the sum of £30,000. These gifts are PETs.

Year Two: no transfers made.

Year Three: Mrs Jones gives her elder daughter £3,000 to help pay for a holiday. This is a PET.

161

Year Four: Mrs Jones gives each of her daughters £12,500. These are both PETs.

Year Five: Mrs Jones dies. She made no transfers prior to Year 1.

Tax charges:

Year One: the three PETs of £30,000 each become chargeable transfers totalling £90,000. This can be reduced to £84,000 chargeable transfer by using up the £3,000 annual exemption for that year and the £3,000 annual exemption brought forward from the previous year.

Year Three: the £3,000 PET becomes a chargeable transfer but no tax is due as it can be offset against the annual allowance.

Year Four: the £25,000 gift becomes a chargeable transfer. This can be reduced to £22,000 by using the annual allowance.

Tax bill

Chargeable transfers	£106,000
Estate	£210,000
Total taxable	£316,000

Table Three: Mrs Jones' Tax Bill

Band	Tax bill	Tax rate
£90,000	Nil	Nil
£50,000	£15,000	30%
£80,000	£32,000	40%
£96,000	£48,000	50%
£306,000	£95,000	60%

In this case Mrs Jones's estate escapes the top band of inheritance tax which is 60% and applies to those sums over £330,000. Table Three shows you how this bill was calculated.

Cost cutting ideas

So much for the calculations, but are there any ways you can reduce your tax bill? The most obvious route is to make full use of both your tax exemptions and PETs. In the past, several investment companies ran complex schemes which involved making gifts into trusts while still allowing you to benefit financially from this arrangement. These schemes are no longer viable and those set up before March 18, 1986 may well be contested by the Inland Revenue when the policyholder eventually dies.

Another route is to use a whole life policy in conjunction with a simple trust which pays out on your death to produce a tax free lump sum in the hands of the person inheriting your estate roughly equivalent to your potential inheritance tax bill. For example, Mrs Jones in year one could have purchased a life assurance plan which paid out £60,000 on her death to her daughters. This would have cost her around £2,000 per year and since it was a regular financial commitment there would be no tax to pay on her premium payments. On her death the £60,000 payment could be used to help pay the inheritance tax bill.

CHAPTER TWELVE:
ACTION STATIONS

Financial planning is not a process which can ever be complete. In general terms it makes sense to check your financial arrangements each year and see whether any adjustments need to be made. This will take into account any changes in your earnings, tax position, assets as well as tax changes on your investments. New products come onto the market seemingly every day and the rules on the tax treatment of competing investments tends to change at least annually. Every March the Chancellor of the day gets to his (or perhaps in the future, her) feet and explains how he intends to run the economy, announces the general level of taxes on goods and services and any alterations to the future tax treatment of investments and income.

Aside from these general considerations there are certain trigger points which should spur you to revise your financial arrangements. These can be divided roughly into events in your own life and circumstances in the general economy.

Personal trigger points

● Income tax

For most people the biggest bite out of their wealth is income tax. It therefore makes sense at all times to minimise your income tax bill by taking full advantage of tax free investments such as National Savings certificates, personal equity plans and friendly society plans. However, over your life you and perhaps your family's income tax position is likely to alter. It is therefore crucial to make full use of any tax allowances due and to arrange your investments in the most tax efficient way.

If you are in the position where you do not pay income tax then clearly you should choose deposit accounts which pay your interest gross. This means opting for the National Savings Investment Account, a one month's notice account, or offshore high interest accounts from reputable banks such as the major high street banks.

PERSONAL TAX RATES 1987-8

Personal allowances

	1986/7	1987/8
Single person's allowance	£2,335	£2,425
Wife's earned income allowance	£2,335	£2,425
Married man's allowance	£3,655	£3,795
Additional personal allowance	£1,320	£1,370
Widow's bereavement allowance	£1,320	£1,370
Blind person's allowance	£360	£540
Single person's allowance (age 65-79)	£2,850	£2,960
Married age allowance (age 65-79)	£4,505	£4,675
Single age allowance (age 80 and over)	£2,850	£3,070
Married age allowance (age 80 and over)	£4,505	£4,845
Age allowance income limit	£9,400	£9,800
Capital gains tax annual exemption (individuals)	£6,300	£6,600

Income tax rate bands

1986/7		1987/8	
Taxable income £	Rate	Taxable income £	Rate
0-17,200	29%	0-17,900	27%
17,201-20,200	40%	17,901-20,400	40%
20,201-25,400	45%	20,401-25,400	45%
25,401-33,300	50%	25,401-33,300	50%
33,301-41,200	55%	33,301-41,200	55%
Over £41,200	60%	Over £41,200	60%

On the investment front remember you can reclaim the basic rate tax paid on share dividends and unit trust distributions. You may wish to shift some of your investments from those with low income to those paying a higher one, subject of course to your requirements for growth. You should try to avoid packaged investments where the tax treatment is worse than your own. If possible go for direct holdings in shares, personal equity plans or unit trusts rather than life assurance products. Remember that many products which claim to give you a tax free lump sum in fact give you a sum on which tax has already been paid.

Those moving up the tax bracket will want to shift where possible into growth orientated investments where they can cash in some of their money if they need income without the money being subject to income tax. Each taxpayer has an annual capital gains tax allowance which after taking account of the rules on indexation means you do not pay tax on gains which simply match inflation.

● Capital gains tax

Think before you sell a major asset. Although gains from your main UK residence are tax free, the tax man takes his bite out of your profits on a second home, antiques, other property, shares, unit trusts etc. It makes sense to try and spread the sales out over the years and to take full advantage of your annual capital gains tax allowance as this cannot be brought forward into future years. For the tax year 1987/8 your allowance is £6,600.

● Additional earned income

If you are in a job which is based on commission, either in whole or part, you need to keep an eagle eye on your financial arrangements. Your tax bracket may change dramatically. Ideally you should try to take advantage of the new profit related pay scheme which will offer certain tax concessions to employees, providing they are not controlling directors with a material interest in the company. A maximum of £3,000 or 20% of your pay, whichever is lower may be profit related provided the total profit related pay bill accounts for at least 5% of the company's payroll.

Before taking on a second job or if you are on a pension, taking on paid employment, work out the impact on your income tax position. Sometimes the benefits are not worth the extra effort. Other times it may give you a bargaining lever with which to raise your pay level or alter the form in which you receive the benefit.

● Inheriting money

Depending upon the size of the payment involved this could radically alter your finances or merely be a small extra sum of cash to tuck away in the bank or building society. You need to consider your options carefully and if it is a five figure sum you should seek financial advice. Do not rush into any investments and try not to take decisions which cannot be easily reversed, i.e. do not go into long term investments which seem to offer a high return without thoroughly reviewing your financial situation and working out what you would like to do with the money. You need to decide for example whether you wish to invest for income, growth or a mixture of the two.

● Buying your home

On average we now buy a new home every five years and each time we pay out about 5% of the new property's cost to a gaggle of professionals, such as solicitors, surveyors etc. and of course the taxman takes his slice by way of stamp duty. We are also faced with the complex decision of how to finance the acquisition and this can only be decided within the context of your existing financial position and insurance arrangements plus your anticipated position over the next ten years or more.

● Marriage

When you get married you will need to inform the taxman

and your employer. You will be treated as a single tax unit and all correspondence will be via the husband in normal circumstances. The husband will receive the higher married man's allowance and the equivalent of the single person's allowance if his wife is working. You will need to change or indeed make a will. Many people will consider life assurance for the first time and may need to sort out their housing situation.

In the early years you will probably be aiming to build up a cash sum by regular saving and planning your cash carefully. If money is tight remember to cover the basics, life assurance, insuring your home, goods and the mortgage before moving on to more esoteric matters of stocks and shares.

• Children

Quite frankly if most of us stopped to think about the cost the human race would probably be in jeopardy, thankfully most people's earnings tend to rise in line with the cost living even though a baby can put a major strain on the family finances.

You will need to make a new will and if like many British households only the husband has life assurance cover, then you should go out and buy cover for the lady of the house. Make sure you buy sufficient insurance. You may even need more than for the average male breadwinner. Legal and General insurance company reckons you would have to pay a collection of people a total of £19,400 in 1987 to perform the tasks of a wife, mother and homemaker.

If you are a single parent, it makes the same sense to be fully insured and make a will. In this case you can also claim the additional personal allowance.

• Changing jobs

Make sure you work out the most attractive take-home package you can. Look at your pension rights, any loans to cover transport costs, catering and leisure facilities and perhaps still the biggest perk of all, a company car. The most problematic area will probably be your pension position, especially if you are in your mid-forties or older. From January 1988 the situation will improve as you will have the option of choosing between a company's pension scheme or making your own arrangements through a portable personal pension. You will also find it easier to unfreeze any existing entitlements which have built up. However, this greater choice means greater scope for making wise and foolish decisions. You will probably need independent expert advice on this matter based on detailed description of your existing pension arrangements, the new company's plan and the personal pensions on the market. You should also take into account your anticipated future job pattern.

On the whole every time you switch investments you lose a small sum if only to cover administration costs. This is particularly vital with pensions, so if you know you are unlikely to stay with the same employer for the rest of your working life you should take this factor into the equation when weighing up your options.

Apart from those events which most of us are likely to encounter through our lives there are also the more traumatic circumstances such as divorce and redundancy which obviously involve both emotional and financial pain. In both circumstances professional financial advice should be sought.

External events

● End of the tax year

The tax year runs from April 6 through to April 5 the following year. Many tax concessions are only available for a specific tax year, while others may be spread over a number of years. You should try to set aside a weekend in late February to go through your affairs and make sure you have taken maximum advantage of those concessions to which you are entitled. Table Two gives you a checklist.

Table Two: End of Tax Year Checklist

1. Have you made full use of your annual capital gains tax allowance (£6,600 for the year 1987-8)?

....

2. If you have children, have they made full use of their capital gains tax allowance?

....

3. Have you used your annual inheritance tax exemption?

....

Has your partner?

....

4. Have you taken full advantage of the rules on tax-free gifts?

....

5. Have you enjoyed the tax-free investments you are allowed to make in the following type of products?:

    National Savings ....

    Friendly society plans ....

    Personal equity plans ....

    Pensions ....

....

6. Have you made sufficient use of your company car, i.e. driven at least 2,500 business miles to minimise tax liability?

....

7. Can you reduce your tax bill further on your company car by driving more than 18,000 business miles before the end of the tax year?

....

8. Has each member of the family made full use of his or her annual income tax allowance?

Main earner ....

Partner ....

Children ....

● The Budget

Every March the Chancellor of the day tells the House of Commons and the country at large how the country's finances will be run over the forthcoming twelve months. At the same time tax changes on the way competing investments are treated are usually announced, although it may be several months before the small print is clear. These announcements may seem remote and complex but they can have a radical effect on the way you should run your family finances. It is therefore worth reading the financial press and reviewing your investments with your regular financial adviser if you have one.

● Inflation

The two main bugbears for investors are inflation and taxes because each eats away at your return. During the eighties we have enjoyed relatively low rates of price increases and interest rates have been by historical standards very high. In such circumstances you can maintain and even increase the real value of your money by putting it on deposit. Index-linked investments, i.e. those where your return is linked to the rise in the Retail Prices Index have not performed as well as ordinary investments.

However, you should never forget about the inflation and the very real damage it can do to your wealth. Table Three is a brief reminder of how inflation gnaws away at the spending power of your money. The government announces statistics on retail prices each month and you can keep an eye out for these. You should also watch out for the Treasury's

172

pronouncements on the future course of inflation. The important point is to try and detect the overall trend and identify those factors which are likely to cause the economy to overheat.

There are as many theories about the cause of inflation as there are economists but some warning signs to watch out for are:

- interest rates moving up sharply
- a boom in imported goods putting pressure on the balance of payments
- the pound value falling in international terms pushing up the real costs of imports
- wage rises running substantially above current inflation rates
- the government boosting borrowing substantially
- the government embarking on massive spending plans
- commodities, particularly energy, rising in price

Table Three: The Pound's Spending Power

at start of:		
1974	. . . .	£1.00
1975	. . . .	84p
1976	. . . .	64p
1977	. . . .	53p
1978	. . . .	45p
1979	. . . .	41p
1980	. . . .	36p
1981	. . . .	29p
1982	. . . .	26p
1983	. . . .	23p
1984	. . . .	22p
1985	. . . .	21p
1986	. . . .	20p

Value of the pound)
(devalued yearly by the percentage fall in the Retail Prices Index)

173

- government action which is likely to cause unease among foreign investors and result in a run on the pound and withdrawal of overseas money
- substantially higher taxes on goods and services

● Stock market

One way or another, be it through your pension, insurance policy, unit trust or investment bond, the value of your savings are probably closely linked to the fortunes of the London stock market and increasingly a number of stock markets around the world. You need therefore to pay attention to what is happening both in the economy in general and the way sentiments about future economic conditions are translated into stock market prices. Remember stock markets tend to reflect people's view of future events, rather than the present, and the herd instinct is very strong. Market price movements often have everything to do with human psychology and virtually little to do with economic realities.

You will need to pay particular attention if you own unit trusts, investment bonds, personal equity plans, a personal pension or a unit linked endowment policy. Stock markets nowadays are much more volatile than they used to be. While it is still true that over time it has paid to stay invested in shares and ride out the storms, however ghastly they were, over specific short term periods this has not been the case. That said, if you have a plan or policy of any sort which is invested indirectly or directly in shares and it is due to mature within the next few years you should keep your eyes peeled and take advice if you are concerned.

While many people say we are now in a sustained phase of rising share prices there is only one thing we can know for certain about the future – that it will be different from the past. So as the boyscouts would say, stay alert.

● Property

As with the stockmarket do not be lulled into a false sense of security. Athough property is traditionally regarded as one of the safest forms of investment you cannot borrow up to the hilt and assume you will make a giant profit. Try to think through the reasons why property prices are rising and then watch out for changes in any of those features. The pull of the South East with its growing employment prospects is obviously fuelling a boom in that region in middle priced homes but the influx of foreign investors has been reduced making homes at the very top end of the market less easy to sell. Mortgage money is flowing like the proverbial wine and honey so this is also pushing up demand.

However, many commentators already see some signs of strain. Growing debt burdens on families who have been sold expensive credit, sometimes by irresponsible lenders, plus a rise in mortgage arrears, often related to the break up of families. Similarly changing patterns of family life will alter the demand for homes of certain sizes and changes in the cost of fuel may have an impact on the price of property in the suburbs. New roads can open up whole areas to commuters as can improved rail links.

• Commodities

As anyone who remembers the 1973 oil crisis can tell you the cost of fuel is vitally important in an industrial society. It therefore makes sense to keep an eye on this, particularly as sterling is regarded in the eyes of the world as a petrocurrency. This means if the price of oil falls, sterling's international buying power tends to nosedive alongside it and vice versa. The Treasury produced information a few years ago showing the impact of oil prices across the economy was fairly neutral, but this seems to cut little ice with international money dealers who buy and sell the world's currencies for a living.

• Political

Changes in government both here and abroad obviously have an impact on your investments. In financial terms the world is now a very small place and in order to attract vital overseas funds we have to be seen to be offering not just an attractive rate of return but a safe haven within an orderly and favourable tax environment. With political change it is a matter of people's perceptions rather than reality. Investors do not hang around to see whether their fears are groundless, they act quickly. This itself can cause a destabilising effect on the economy and often precipitate the events people feared in the first place.

- Exchange controls

In 1979 the Thatcher government removed restrictions on UK residents investing overseas and in the 1987 Budget announced plans to remove the law which established exchange controls from the statute book. Any plans to reintroduce exchange controls or rumours about the reimposition would obviously effect the flow of funds into London and result in a rush of money offshore. It could also effect the return on insurance, pension and other investments if they were forced to repatriate money or were penalised with higher tax rates for holding overseas investments.

- Moves to encourage equity investment

Much of the Renaissance of European stockmarkets and the continued rise in world markets can be placed firmly at the doorstep of governments around the world. They have encouraged people to put money in shares by giving tax incentives, altering the relative tax treatment of equity investments versus other types and tried to persuade people to take control of their own savings rather than rely on state payments which are funded by taxes. In terms of sheer size moves to encourage people to finance their own pensions, where much of the money will be invested in shares, are probably the most important.

USEFUL ADDRESSES

Accepting Houses
Committee
Granite House
101 Cannon Street
London EC4N 5BA
Tel: (01) 283 7332

Advertising Standards
Authority (ASA)
Brook House
2-16 Torrington Place
London WC1E 7HN
Tel: (01) 580 5555

Associated Scottish Life
Offices
23 St. Andrews Square
Edinburgh EH2 1AQ
Tel: (031) 556 7171

Association of British
Insurers
Aldermary House
Queen Street
London EC4N 1TT
Tel: (01) 248 4477

Association of British Travel
Agents (ABTA)
55-57 Newman Street
London W1P 4AH
Tel: (01) 637 2444

Association of Certified
Accountants
29 Lincoln's Inn Fields
London WC2A 3EE
Tel: (01) 242 6855

Association of Futures
Brokers and Dealers
(AFBD)
Cereal House
58 Mark Lane
London EC3R 7NE
Tel: (01) 488 0898

Association of Investment
Trust Companies
6th Floor Park House
16 Finsbury Circus
London EC2M 7JP
Tel: (01) 588 5347

Association of Mail Order
Publishers
1 New Burlington Street
London W1X 1FD
Tel: (01) 437 0706

Banking Information Service
10 Lombard Street
London EC3V 9AR
Tel: (01) 626 8486

Bank of England
Threadneedle Street
London EC2R 8AH
Tel: (01) 601 4444

Barclays Bank PLC
54 Lombard Street
London EC3P 3AH
Tel: (01) 636 1567

British Insurance Brokers
Association (BIBA)
14 Bevis Marks
London EC3A 7NT
Tel: (01) 623 9043

Building Employers
Confederation
82 New Cavendish Street
London W1N 8AD
Tel: (01) 580 5588

Building Societies
Association
3 Savile Row
London W1X 1AF
Tel: (01) 437 0655

Building Society
Commission
15/17 Great Marlborough
Street
London W1V 2AX
Tel: (01) 437 9992

Chartered Institute of
Arbitrators
75 Cannon Street
London EC4N 5BH
Tel: (01) 236 8761

Chartered Institute of Public
Finance and Accountancy
1 Buckingham Place
London SW1E 6HS

CCN Systems Ltd
Talbot House
Talbot Street
Nottingham NG1 5HS
Tel: 0602-410888

Citizens' Advice Bureaux
(National Association)
115-123 Pentonville Road
London N1 9L2
Tel: (01) 833 2181

Company Pensions
Information Centre
7 Old Park Lane
London W1Y 3LJ
Tel: (01) 409 1933

Consumers' Association
14 Buckingham Street
London WC2N 6DS
Tel: (01) 839 1222

Corporation of Insurance
and Financial Advisers
6/7 Leapale Road
Guildford
Surrey GU1 4JX
Tel: (0483) 39121

Inland Revenue
Somerset House
Strand
London WC2R 1LB
Tel: (01) 438 6622

Institute of Chartered
Accountants in England and
Wales
Chartered Accountants Hall
Moorgate Place
London EC2P 2BJ
Tel: (01) 628 7060

Institute of Chartered
Accountants of Scotland
27 Queen Street
Edinburgh EH2 1LA
Tel: (031) 225 5673

Institute of Cost and
Management Accountants
63 Portland Place
London W1N 4AB
Tel: (01) 580 6542

Institute of Chartered
Secretaries and
Administrators
16 Park Crescent
London W1N 4AH
Tel: (01) 580 4741

Institute of Insurance
Consultants
PO Box 231
121A Queensway, Bletchley,
Milton Keynes MK1 1X2
Tel: (0908) 643364

Insurance Brokers
Registration Council
15 St. Helens Place
London EC3A 6DS
Tel: (01) 588 4387

Department of Trade and
Industry
1 Victoria Street
London SW1H 0ET
Tel: (01) 215 7877

Financial Intermediaries,
Managers and Brokers
Regulatory Association
(FIMBRA)
22 Great Tower Street
London EC3R 5AQ
Tel: (01) 283 4814

Finance Houses Association
18 Upper Grosvenor Street
London W1X 9PB
Tel: (01) 491 2783

Incorporated Society of
Valuers and Auctioneers
3 Cadogan Gate
London SW1X 0AS
Tel: (01) 235 2282

Industrial Life Offices
Association
Aldermary House
10-15 Queen Street
London EC4N 1TL
Tel: (01) 248 4477

International Securities
Regulatory Organisation
(ISRO)
2nd Floor 45 London Wall
London EC2M 5TE
Tel: (01) 256 8823

Investment Management
Regulatory Organisation
(IMRO)
45 London Wall
London EC2M 5TE
Tel: (01) 256 7261

Land Registry
32 Lincoln's Inn Fields
London WC2A 3PH
Tel: (01) 405 3488

Law Society
113 Chancery Lane
London WC2A 1PL
Tel: (01) 242 1222

Life Assurance and Unit
Trust Regulatory
Organisation (LAUTRO)
Aldermary House
Queen Street
London EC4N 1TP
Tel: (01) 248 4477

Life Insurance Association
Citadel House
Station Approach
Chorleywood
Herts
Tel: (09278) 5333

Lloyds Bank PLC
71 Lombard Street
London EC3P 3BS
Tel: (01) 626 1500

Mail Order Traders
Association
25 Castle Street
Liverpool 2
Tel: (051) 227 4181

Midland Bank PLC
Poultry
London EC2P 2BX
Tel: (01) 606 9911

National Association of
Conveyancers
2 Chichester Rents
40 Chancery Lane
London WC2A 1EG
Tel: (01) 404 5737

National Association of
Estate Agents
21 Jury Street
Warwick CV34 4EH
Tel: (0926) 496800

National Association of
Pension Funds
12-18 Grosvenor Gardens
London SW1W 0DH
Tel: (01) 730 0585

National Girobank
Bridle Road
Bootle
Merseyside G1R 0AA
Tel: (051) 928 8181

National House Building
Council
58 Portland Place
London W1N 4BU
Tel: (01) 637 1248

Newspaper Publishers'
Association Ltd.
6 Bouverie Street
London EC4Y 8OY
Tel: (01) 583 8132

National Westminster Bank
PLC
41 Lothbury
London EC2P 2BP
Tel: (01) 606 6060

Newspaper Society
Whitefriar House
6 Carmelite Street
London EC4Y 0BL
Tel: (01) 583 3311

Occupational Pensions
Advisory Service
Room 327, Aviation House
129 Kingsway
London WC2B 6NN
Tel:

Occupational Pensions
Board
Lynwood Road
Thames Ditton
Surrey KT7 0DP
Tel: (01) 398 4242

Office of Fair Trading
Field House
15-25 Bream's Buildings
London EC4A 1PR
Tel: (01) 242 2858

OMBUDSMEN
Parliamentary
Commissioner and Health
Service Commissioner
Church House
Great Smith Street
London SW1P 3BW
Tel: (01) 212 7676

Insurance Ombudsman
Bureau
31 Southampton Row
London WC1B 5HJ
Tel: (01) 242 8613

Commissioners for Local
Administration
Greater London, South
East, South West, W.
Midlands,
East Anglia
21 Queen Anne's Gate
London SW1H 9BU
Tel: (01) 222 5622

North and East Midlands
29 Castlegate
York YO1 1RN
Tel: (0904) 30151

Scotland
5 Shandwick Place
Edinburgh EH2 4RG
Tel: (031) 229 4472

Wales
Derwen House
Court Road
Bridgend
Mid-Glamorgan CF31 1BN
Tel: (0656) 61325

Office of the Banking
Ombudsman
Citadel House
5/11 Fetter Lane
London EC4A 1BR
Tel: (01) 583 1395

Personal Insurance
Arbitration Service
75 Cannon Street
London EC4N 5BH
Tel: (01) 236 8761

Royal Institute of British
Architects (RIBA)
66 Portland Place
London W1N 4AD
Tel: (01) 580 5533

Royal Institute of Chartered
Surveyors (RICS)
12 Great George Street
Parliament Square
London SW1P 3AD
Tel: (01) 222 7000

Securities and Investment
Board (SIB)
3 Royal Exchange Buildings
London EC3V 3NL
Tel: (01) 283 2474

Society of Pension
Consultants
Ludgate House
Ludgate Circus
London EC4A 2AB
Tel: (01) 353 1688

Solicitors Complaints
Bureau
Stock Exchange
Old Broad Street
London EC2N 1HP
Tel: (01) 588 2355

Trustee Savings Bank
PO Box 41
49-53 Surrey Row
London SE1 0BY
Tel: (01) 633 9344

Unit Trust Association
Park House
16 Finsbury Circus
London EC2M 7JP
Tel: (01) 628 0871

United Association for the
Protection of Trade (UAPT)
Zodiac House
163 London Road
Croydon
Tel: (01) 686 5644

Index

ALSO AVAILABLE FROM ROSTERS LTD

THE SHARE BOOK (2nd Edn)
By Rosemary Burr

The new enlarged version of this national bestseller is packed full of practical advice and hints on choosing a reputable stockbroker, picking the right shares to suit your needs and explains your rights as a shareholder. 'A valuable source of information and advice' writes The Prime Minister Margaret Thatcher in the book's introduction. Plus, full list of shareholders' perks, top 100 companies in the country and members of the Stock Exchange.

ISBN 0 948032 65 0   Hardback   Price: £8.95

GUIDE TO PERSONAL EQUITY PLANS
By Rosemary Burr

How to benefit from the new tax free schemes. The book explains the details of the schemes and analyses the charges and investment policies of the competing plans. You can only invest in one Personal Equity Plan each year, this book will help you make the right choice.

ISBN 0 948032 70 7   Price: £3.99

UNIT TRUSTS EXPLAINED
By Rosemary Burr

Unit trusts provide a simple and cost effective way of investing in shares around the world as well as here at home. This book shows you how to take advantage of unit trusts whether you are looking for income or capital growth. It discusses various strategies designed to help you pick high flying trusts and shows how you can incorporate unit trusts into your general financial plan.

ISBN 0 948032 40 5   Price: £3.99

MORE SHARES FOR YOUR MONEY
By Christine Stopp

Sponsored by the Association of Investment Trust Companies this is a handy guide to the potentially profitable world of investment trust companies. It explains what sort of return you can expect from your share investment and describes the wide variety of trusts which you can use to generate income or capital growth. Plus a list of stockbrokers who are prepared to give recommendations, tips on planning your portfolio and a glossary to help you understand the jargon.
ISBN 0 948032 90 1   Price: £5.95

FEMALE TYCOONS
By Rosemary Burr

Interviews 12 of Britain's top businesswomen who reveal the secrets of their success. Includes: Anita Roddick of The Body Shop, The 1987 Businesswoman of the Year, Jennifer Rosenburg and Britt Allcroft, the lady behind Thomas the Tank.
ISBN 0 948032 75 8   Price: £4.95

SUN, SAND AND CEMENT
By Cheryl Taylor

A comprehensive guide to buying a property overseas. How to overcome the pitfalls plus popular spots for the retired, those with families, singles and those seeking an income.
ISBN 0 948032 45 6   Price: £5.99

FUNNY MONEY
By Alan Ralph

If you thought money was no laughing matter, this book will change your mind. Witty and incisive cartoons to put a smile on your face.

ISBN 0 948032 20 0   Price: £2.95

STAR QUALITY
By Marjorie Orr

The first astrology book to show you how to maximise your potential – be it at home or at work.

ISBN 0 948032 35 9   Price: £4.95

ABBEY FINANCIAL RIGHTS HANDBOOK
By Wendy Elkington

How not to get ripped off by your bank, building society, insurance broker or investment adviser. Tips to beat the hard sell and vital information on your rights, how to get redress and ways of checking a financial adviser's credentials. An essential handbook for all consumers.

ISBN 0 948032 80 4   Price: £5.95

INVESTORS A-Z
Edited by Rosemary Burr

Essential reading for savers and investors. More than 700 terms explained simply and concisely. A vital reference book before you start shopping for insurance or investment plans.

ISBN 6 948032 55 3   Price: £5.99

THE PRUDENTIAL BOOK OF MONEY
Edited by Rosemary Burr

A comprehensive guide to solving your money problems.
Written by ten of the country's leading financial journalists
it tackles issues ranging from how to budget, buying the
correct amount and type of insurance, investing for income
or growth, picking the right pension and enjoyiung the fruits
of a tax free personal equity plan.
ISBN 0 948032 60 X   Price: £3.50

MAKE YOUR PENSION WORK
Edited by Rosemary Burr

How to take advantage of tax free pensions and the new
freedom from January 1988 to make your own pension
arrangements. Making sure you get your full state pension,
weighing up the options of buying a personal pension versus
staying in an occupational scheme, using your pension to cut
your tax bill and pay for your home.
ISBN 0 948032 50 2   Price: £5.95

SLOBS GUIDE TO GOOD LIVING
By Rosemary Burr, Hilary Dolling and Tracy Jeune
Cartoons: Nigel Paige

Forget about becoming a jogging fiend, health guru or a
tailor's dummy being a slob is much more fun. Looks at slobs
through history, their pleasures, pursuits and watering holes.
ISBN 0 948032 21 9   Price: £4.95